Creating T2 'the book' has meant we could tell the story about how we do tea differently. What it is that T2 does that makes us unique.

The T2 story is one of passion, reinvention and breaking the rules with a creative focus.

This is not a book on how to build a brand or business — it is a book about taking

For more, go to T2tea.com

one of the world's oldest beverages and making it young and effervescent, creating a new generation of tea drinkers globally.

We will walk you through the T2 essentials on how to enjoy tea ... every day in every way.

Enjoy every sip ! — MaryAnne x

I dedicate
this book to the T2
team — over the years
we have grown to be
a tea loving, brewing,
drinking force
around the world and
your passion for T2
and what we do
inspires me daily.

Thank you!

2

the book

Maryanne Shearer

LANTERN

an imprint of
PENGUIN BOOKS

13

A moment's
pause in a
busy day

Sip
& Slurp 77

Make
It 12

Introduction 1

T2™
THE BOOK

CONTENTS

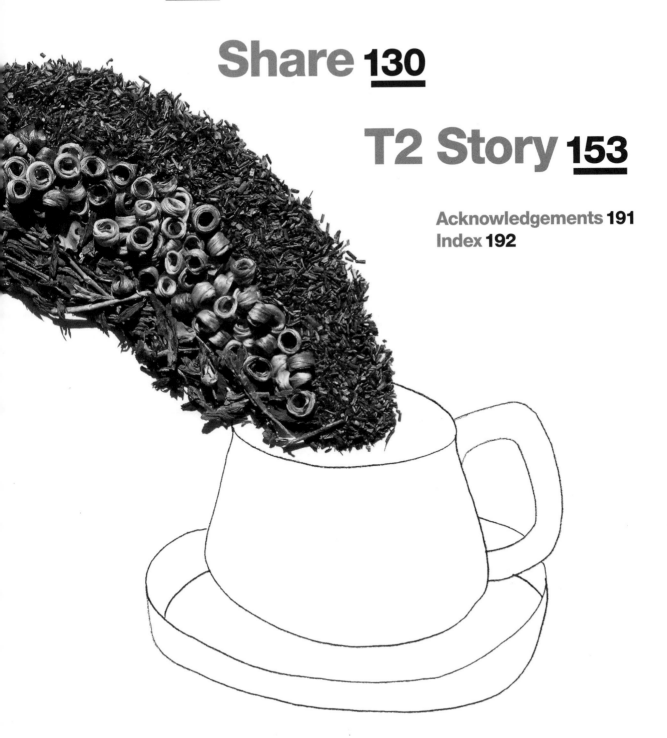

Eat 107

Share 130

T2 Story 153

Acknowledgements 191
Index 192

Introduction

Early days

When I was growing up my passion was for making things: anything using my imagination and my hands. That turned into a passion for fashion, and I always imagined that I would become a designer, or at least work in the fashion industry in some way.

I inherited my creativity from both my father and my grandfather: I remember I used to sit for hours and watch my grandfather draw and paint, and I have always found beautiful things inspiring and intriguing. My mother always worked very hard and long hours, and I definitely inherited my work ethic from her.

I didn't have the patience for school; I was a very average student, definitely a dreamer. I was really keen to get out into the big wide world and start to make a difference, so I left school quite early. I then got a job with a fashion retailer, Cherry Lane, in visual merchandising. This was perfect for me; I was using all of my creative skills and I was getting paid for it. I learned to create a sense of theatre for the customer – something I still love doing. I spent about three years at Cherry Lane, by which time I was buying and styling, and had developed an absolute affinity for retail.

From there I joined fashion retailer JAG, and then after a couple of years at JAG I joined a company that supplied retailers with visual merchandising and shop-fitting product. I was employed as the company's fashion consultant, working with their fashion retail clients. I really enjoyed dealing with such a diverse group of retailers and spent 8 years there.

Starting a business

It was through that job that I met T2 co-founder Jan O'Connor. We had a lot in common and decided to go into business together. Our original plan was to start a homewares company, and in 1995 we registered a company called Contents Homeware.

We took off on a buying trip around the world and while in New York we came across a great tea-based product called Water Leaf. While in Europe we had also, quite unintentionally, purchased a lot of homeware samples that were all tea related. We didn't realise it at the time, but this was the beginning of our incredible tea journey.

One day, Jan and I were chatting about the fact that there were lots of coffee shops opening up, but no tea shops. We looked at each other and that was it: tea. No one was doing tea. Our eyes lit up and we knew it would work. We were definitely on to something! We needed a name, so we thought, 'there are two of us, and tea plus two works'. 'Tea two' was just a little predictable so we spelled the 'two' as 'too', just because we could. After a while, Tea Too became T2: it helped that it was quicker to write and it looked good.

We headed to what we felt was the most happening Melbourne suburb – Fitzroy, which we thought would be the perfect location for our store, and found a great space for lease. Now, Jan and I got to work planning and organising our new tea retail world.

We were working out of Jan's apartment at the time and we met every morning to fill each other in on our progress. Initially, we weren't able to persuade anyone to finance us – everyone we approached thought we were mad. However, Jan and I were completely convinced of what we were doing and both put our personal savings on the line. We did everything on

This page shows our early accidental approach to merchandising. The image on the far right shows our new look – still busy, but a sense of order was needed to help the customer navigate such a diverse collection of products.

a shoestring budget and roped in our family and friends to help us pull the first store together.

Visual merchandising was vitally important from the start and we set out to offer a complete sensory experience. Black was chosen as our signature colour, giving the stores a backdrop for the theatre we wanted to create. We also wanted our store to have an Oriental feel about it – it was our way of paying homage to China and the role it had played in the history of tea, so we used old Chinese newspaper to cover up the less-than-perfect walls of the Fitzroy store. Black walls and units, Chinese newspaper on the walls and splashes of colour established a distinct look for T2 stores,

and even now black is part of our company culture; everyone at T2 wears black – it unites us.

Back in those early days, the first thing we needed to do was to find a reliable supplier of tea, and in Bill Bennett of tea importers HA Bennett & Sons, we found so much more than just a supplier. He became our mentor, and was an endless source of advice and encouragement. He invited us into the world of tea – its history, its politics and its romance. We began to realise that there is much more to tea than just a box of leaves on a supermarket shelf and we always left meetings with him full of ideas and renewed enthusiasm.

Our main aim was for a retail environment that offered passion and a sense of theatre. We wanted our store to not only look good, but also to smell good and taste good. We felt it was important that we had tea leaves on display so the customer could play with them and actually see the varieties available. Very few retail stores were offering samples or tastings, and this became one of our many points of difference. Our tastings helped complete the sensory experience – and we found that, generally, whatever tea we offered for tasting was the tea we would sell the most of. We would spend hours sipping tea and chatting with our customers, learning more and more about tea every day. Education for us and our customers became critical, and it's now an integral part of our culture.

We began by buying tea from Bill in five-kilogram sacks, and using takeaway noodle boxes as our packaging, which were new and exciting back in 1996. All the packaging and bags were stamped by hand with our brand, 'Tea Too Tea'. There were just three short months from our first idea for Tea Too until the opening of our first store on Brunswick Street, on July 1 1996.

At home in Fitzroy

I remember us standing, proudly looking around our store the night before opening day and thinking how great it looked. We ripped open a bag of tea and scattered it over a display of teacups: that tea installation was the beginning of the years of effort we put into our windows. We also thought we might get a lot of customers buying gifts, so we cut up some of the leftover Chinese newspaper from the walls to bind the noodle boxes. Eighteen years later, we are still using the Chinese newspaper concept in our wrapping. The noodle box was superseded after six or seven years by an orange cardboard cube and this, together with our orange carry bag, has become one of the most important symbols of T2.

On the first day of trade, we had forty teas for sale (today we have over 200), and it was just Jan and me in the store, with our mums out the back packing tea for us. We took $420 in sales– not enough to cover wages or rent – but we were in business. Customers loved our concept from day one. That doesn't mean that the business was a commercial success straight away. In fact, it took us years to make money, but the brand was strong from that first day in Fitzroy.

The early days were incredibly hectic. The more tea we sold, the more shelves there were to restock at night, and the more tea to be packed.

Our early stores had a very strong Chinese theme, paying homage to the part China played in the history of tea. These are a couple of early team shots, one at the opening of our Bondi store, the other at our fancy dress Christmas party.

We spent our days in the store, making tea for our customers and ourselves, and our nights packing tea, ready for the next day's trade.

As our business grew, so did our confidence, and a year after we opened in Brunswick Street, we opened a second store on Fitzroy Street, St Kilda. Unfortunately it didn't meet with the same success as our original store. Although the premises were perfect, there weren't enough customers coming through the door and after 12 months, we had to close the doors. We learned a valuable lesson: retail really is all about location.

The Chadstone store

After our St Kilda experience, we were quite happy to stay put with our Fitzroy store for a while. We had been able to start employing paid team members, and had also started supplying our teas to restaurants and cafés. We leased an area above the Fitzroy store to use as an office. However, in 1998, we were approached to open a store in Chadstone shopping centre, the largest in Australia. The centre was undergoing major expansion and the leasing team there were very persuasive and so passionate about what we were doing that they convinced us that a T2 store would work well as part of the development. We were naturally quite apprehensive.

Our Chadstone store opened in November 1999 and took off straight away. In fact, Chadstone was selling more tea than we could keep up with. During the first Christmas we had with Chadstone open, we ran out of stock in both stores. Every time we got a delivery of more product, it would sell out, and both stores were full of customers who were unhappy about the empty shelves and team members who were exhausted.

Like many new and small businesses, our problem became one of cash flow. We needed more money if we were going to open more stores of Chadstone's calibre. It was at this point that my partner, Bruce Crome, stepped in to help. He is an engineer by trade, who had run his own successful business for many years. He had lent the business money over the years, but this time he provided us with a formal loan, and also engaged professional accountants to help us to streamline our finances.

Three babies in fifteen months

As well as running a burgeoning business, I was about to experience significant change in my private life, too. In March 2000, our first child, Hannah, was born. I returned to work when she was just five weeks old, taking her in to the office with me every day. Unfortunately, at this time my business relationship with Jan was starting to deteriorate. We had worked together for almost four years, and although T2 was trading well, the challenges of running a start-up were taking their toll on our partnership.

The Chadstone store was extremely busy every day, and with limited team members to help out, the burden fell on both of us. Our mothers and friends were working full-time for very little return, just to keep the stock on the shelves. Meanwhile, five months after I had Hannah, I was pregnant again – this time with twins!

Oliver and Harry were born in 2001, about eighteen months after Chadstone opened. Bruce, my partner, had retired, so I would leave Hannah at home with him and a nanny, and bring Oliver and Harry into work with me. My mum came to work with us and helped me as much as she could with the boys, but my days were a fog of working really hard, and coping with my beautiful newborn twins and Hannah. Relations between Jan and myself continued to be strained, and we bought out her share of the business when the boys were just a few months old. Now I really needed help.

I called my sister Kirsten, who is 12 years younger than me and was working in the rag trade. I told her that I desperately needed her to join T2 to get me through this really tricky time. From the day Kirsten started, she changed the focus of the business. Over the years, I had become increasingly consumed with the growth of the business, the product and what we offered, and had probably not paid enough attention to customer service. Kirsten introduced customer service at such a high level that the customers fell in love all over again. This was great, but it meant we were even busier!

This is a shot of the gang, Hannah upfront, Ollie and Harry clearly more interested in the camera than what I was trying to explain to them, and Bruce Crome, my partner.

Beyond Melbourne

By 2001 T2 was ready to open a store in Sydney, so Kirsten and I jumped on a plane to have a look around. We found a little store in Newtown, a location that reminded us very much of Fitzroy. Sydney store number one was on its way.

At this stage we couldn't afford to travel overseas, and I was still buying all the homewares and most of the tea in Australia through agents. We were buying some teas from overseas agents and our customers were still pretty keen on basic teas, such as English Breakfast. Our customers were enjoying the service, the beautiful brews and the gift wrapping, and we were also blending the teas ourselves. As our customers' palates became more adventurous we began to make our own blends based on their feedback. This was a critical part of our decision to carry a greater variety of teas, as our customers really love to be surprised. Every time our customers visited the stores they would discover a new blend to add to their collection.

Over the next few years we opened about one store a year and enjoyed a slow and steady growth, operating six stores by 2004. We then turned our attention to our supply chain. Our customers had become used to a constant supply of new teas and we had implemented seasonal buying cycles for our homewares, just like in fashion. This meant that we had to devote considerable energy to nurturing our suppliers and we demanded a lot of them to help us reinvent our products. The whole T2 team was working ridiculously long hours, but our customers loved what we were doing, and this helped to spur us on.

The image on the left shows our Newtown store, our first store in Sydney. At right, Kirsten and me at the opening in 2001.

Reinvention

We realised we needed to reinvent ourselves, as our customers demanded even more tea varieties. Our homewares, too, were lacking a point of difference. We had lost some of our creative focus. My sister Kirsten was running the stores and looking after the customer experience, and I had employed Nicholas Beckett as our CFO. My responsibility was product and brand development together with location selection, as I believed (and still do) that this is one of the most important decisions a retailer can make.

Reinvention has been one of the keys to success for T2, both in regard to the in-store experience and the business. By 2005 we had eight stores, fifty-five team members and were turning over 4.4 million dollars. The following year we nearly doubled our turnover, taking it to 8 million dollars. We were growing at a lightning pace.

While I was able to focus completely on growing the business and protecting the brand, Kirsten and Nicholas concentrated on running their areas of the business. This three-pronged approach, together with Bruce's financial support, worked magically for more than 10 years.

We continued to open stores in all states across Australia and in New Zealand. Our wholesale tea business became a critical part of our branding growth strategy and online sales also started to multiply.

In 2012 we were being approached by a number of large companies interested in buying us out. Bruce and I decided it was probably time to seriously consider selling the business. We were getting enquiries from international retailers almost daily about expanding into their territories, and we needed to partner with a company with the network and financial clout required to take our unique brand to the rest of the world.

In October 2013, Unilever acquired T2. Unilever is actually the world's largest tea company and it was very keen to support us. As I write this in early 2015, T2 now comprises sixty-eight retail outlets, including stores

Our first store in the US, in downtown Soho. It was so important that we opened in New York using the 'best of' to help establish us in a new market.

in London and New York. We have more than 900 employees, 600,000 members in our Tea Society loyalty program, over 75,000 Facebook followers and 30,000 people are engaged with us on Instagram. My role since T2 changed ownership is that of Creative Director and I still look forward to going into work at T2 every single day and coming up with exciting and innovative ways to bring tea to the world. I am in awe of what we have created. ■

T2 HQ is our temp
tea. It's a comfort
place, more like a
home than an offi
where we can all
what we do best
in peace and calm
or creative chaos

Tea makes everything better... everything is ok when you are having a cup of tea!
– Kirsten Shearer

Tea is an experience; it's the smell, it's the feel, it's the taste It is something that brings people from all different walks of life together.
– Scott Yurisich

What is

Tea for me is a time to stop, sip and let go.
– Jaime Ireland

Tea is a small sojourn in your day –
Heath Barrett

tea is a moment of
peacefulness and calm
— Jessica Tate.

Tea is moments of joy in a cup
and memories and something to share
with those you love ♥
— Kate Iles

Tea is the
"coming together
of family + friends".
A sip at life that
lingers an the palate.
Tea is the afternoon glow
+ the morning screech of
the bubbling kettle.
— Meredith O'Neil

A simple pleasure
that comes in many forms.
An excuse to stop and
draw breath in a crazy
world — Nick Beckett.

What is tea?

Wherever you go in the world – from the highest mountains of the Himalayas to the deserts of the Sahara, from the Antarctic to the beaches of Ecuador, you will be offered a cup of tea.

A cup of tea welcomes a guest and marks the end of a meal. It warms you up when you are cold and cools you down when it's too hot. Tea has been drunk for thousands of years, has its own history and arcane customs and is so highly valued that wars have been fought in its name.

Like a glass of wine, every cup of tea tells its own story. The flavour of the tea changes according to the soil in which the tree was grown, the rainfall and sunshine of that season, the method of leaf picking and, of course, the process by which it ended up in your pot. All of these factors go towards making each cup of tea unique.

There are hundreds of types of tea, but each one comes from the same base. All tea is made from the leaves of the camellia tree; there are 200 species of camellia, but only one – *Camellia sinensis* – is used to produce tea. This species has three main varieties: *sinensis*, *assamica* and *cambodgiensis*. Most tea comes from the *sinensis* varietal, which has a strong resistance to cold weather and dry conditions, and so thrives at high altitudes.

Trees of the *assamica* variety have less aromatic leaves, which produce a darker, more robust liquid. Leaves from the *cambodgiensis* variety are rarely used for tea cultivation, but the plant is often hybridised with the other two.

It takes 5 kilos of fresh leaves, or about 12,000 shoots, to produce 1 kilo of tea. Most tea pickers will harvest about 30 to 50 kilos of tea per day.

Picking tea is a very delicate operation that, when it is done by hand, is almost always performed by women, due to their smaller fingers. The timing is absolutely critical – younger leaves have more aromatic compounds, but they are smaller than older leaves. So the tea plantation owner must find a balance between the quality of the tea harvested and the quantity of leaves produced. Because the delicate leaves from the first harvest of the year contain the highest concentration of aromatic oils, they are the most valuable. For instance, Darjeeling First Flush, which comes from the first harvests of the finest plantations of Darjeeling, is keenly anticipated by tea aficionados and is collected like fine wines.

When tea leaves go through their final sorting and grading, they get special names. There are two main grades of tea – leaf and broken leaf. Broken-leaf teas are not necessarily lower quality; they are simply processed differently and produce a stronger-flavoured liquid. 'Dust' or 'fannings' teas are made from crushed leaves and because of this, they are normally sold in teabags.

Tea leaves are graded as variations of the term 'orange pekoe', which refers to the fine picking of a later harvest. The most prestigious type of picking, superfine picking, involves taking just the bud and the leaf below it. Fine picking harvests the bud and the first two leaves, and medium picking is the bud plus three leaves.

The word pekoe comes from the Chinese *pak-ho*, which is the fine downy hair on the body of a newborn baby. Thus pekoe refers to the young tea buds that are covered with a fine down. The word orange has nothing to do with colour, but refers to the Dutch royal family, known as the House of Orange. This term was probably first used by Dutch tea merchants to convey royal patronage.

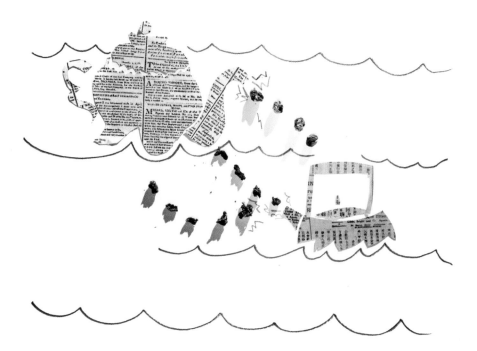

Opium Wars or Tea Wars?

The trade in tea was such an important part of the Opium Wars between China and the West that some historians believe they should be renamed the Tea Wars.

Before the 1830s, only one port – Canton (Guangzhou) – was open to Western merchants, and the Chinese government insisted on being paid in silver. This was a problem for Britain and America, because they were importing huge quantities of tea, porcelain, cotton and silk from China but lacked the silver to pay for it. To make up for this, they found the one product that the Chinese wanted but did not make themselves, which was opium.

The British trading houses bought opium in India and sent it to Canton. By the late 1830s, more than 30,000 chests were being imported annually. The effect of all this opium on the Chinese people and the economy was devastating – up to 90 per cent of all Chinese men under the age of 40 were spending their days in an opiate haze, and business and the civil service almost ground to a halt.

By 1839, the Chinese Emperor had sent a special emissary, Lin Ze-xu, to Canton to sort out the problem. He arrested 1600 foreign merchants and confiscated and publicly burnt all the opium he could find, which was worth millions of dollars. Finally, he ordered the port of Canton to be closed to all foreign merchants. In retaliation, the British chief superintendent of trade, Charles Elliott, ordered a blockade of the Pearl River and there was a long naval battle, marking the start of the first Opium War.

The superior British navy overwhelmed the Chinese, and by 1842 Britain had taken control of Canton and its surrounding area. Under the terms of the Treaty of Nanking, China gave the island of Hong Kong to Britain, opened five ports to Western trade, granted Britain a 'most favoured nation' trade status and paid $US9 million compensation for the destroyed opium. In addition, China was required to abolish trading monopolies and limit tariffs.

Britain continued to push for more concessions from the Chinese government and relations between the two countries became more and more strained. In 1856, Chinese officials, suspecting smuggling and piracy, boarded a Hong Kong-based merchant ship and arrested several of the sailors. The British and American governments weren't happy, and the following year they sent warships to Canton, where they were joined by French and Russian troops. This marked the start of the second Opium War.

The Western forces won again and by 1860 the Chinese government had signed the Convention of Peking, which included giving the port of Kowloon to Britain and allowing indentured Chinese labourers to emigrate to America. It is often said that without these workers, the huge railways of the United States and Canada would not have been completed so quickly and cheaply.

Boston Tea Party

The English immigrants to America took their tea-drinking habits with them and by the eighteenth century upwardly mobile Americans were having elaborate tea parties with silver teapots and porcelain tea sets. More and more people took up the habit and soon one-third of the population drank tea twice a day.

By 1860, tea was the third biggest import to America after textiles and manufactured goods. The British government, impoverished by prolonged wars in France and India, decided to levy heavy taxes on the American colony, which was very unpopular. The colonists believed that they shouldn't be subject to taxes imposed by a British parliament in which they were not represented and 'No taxation without representation!' became the cry.

The British parliament retreated, removing most of the taxes, but maintained a duty on tea. They gave the East India Company a monopoly on the export of tea to America and lowered the rate of duty. This meant the colony would get its tea at a good price, but would have to acknowledge Parliament's right to tax them. The British assumed that the Americans would sacrifice their principles to be able to keep on drinking tea.

The Americans did not back down, however, and when ships carrying tea attempted to land in Philadelphia and New York they were turned away. The Philadelphia protestors said the tea contained the 'seeds of slavery'.

In December 1773, three East India ships arrived in Boston Harbor and a large crowd of people gathered at the port and decided to make the ships leave without paying duty. However, the Collector of Customs refused to allow this. One night, three groups of men, about fifty altogether, dressed up as Mohawk Indians, boarded the ships and took control of its cargo, which was 340 chests of tea. Then, in an incident that became known as the Boston Tea Party, they slashed them open with tomahawks and threw the tea and the chests into the water.

This incident was reported around the world and the British government felt that it could not go unpunished. It closed the port of Boston and enacted other punitive laws known as the Coercive Acts. By 1775, the American War of Independence had broken out but it was 8 years before Britain conceded defeat and granted America its independence. Once again, tea had started a war, which in this case had led to a revolution. But one thing didn't change – Americans continued to drink tea. ▪

T2 world

Creme brulee (a bit French?)

Green Rose

Irish Breakfast →

Just Lavender
Our lavender comes from France

Normal Tea
Because that's what they drink

Yerba Mate
Very popular in
South America

Red
(Rooibos is
from Africa)

We love to create brews
that take you on a journey,
so we travel the planet
to source tea from many
different places. Our view
of the world is tea-skewed,
and looks something like
this ... it's all about tea!

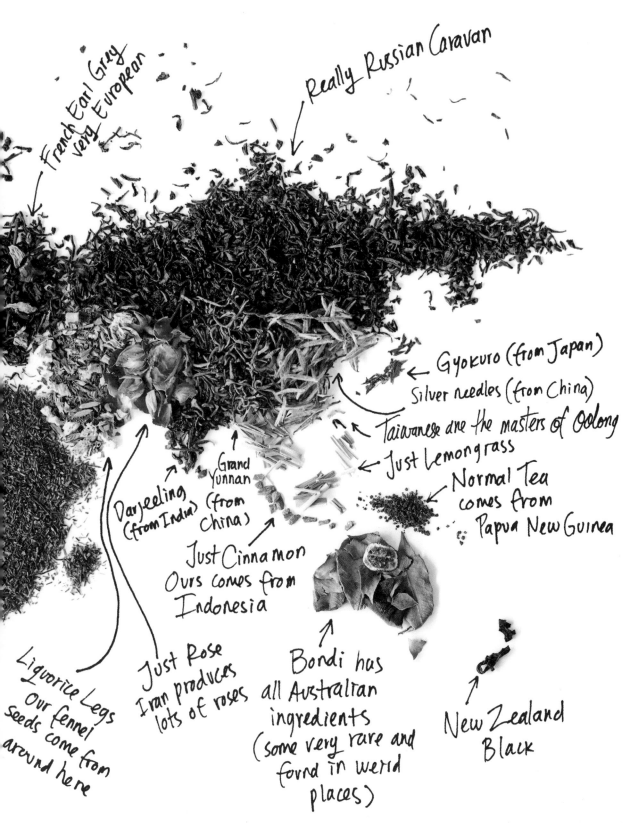

French Earl Grey
very European

Really Russian Caravan

Gyokuro (from Japan)

Silver needles (from China)

Taiwanese are the masters of Oolong

Just Lemongrass

Normal Tea comes from Papua New Guinea

Darjeeling (from India)

Grand Yunnan (from China)

Just Cinnamon
Ours comes from Indonesia

Liquorice Legs
Our fennel seeds come from around here

Just Rose
Iran produces lots of roses

Bondi has all Australian ingredients (some very rare and found in weird places)

New Zealand Black

23

Processing tea

Tea is the most-consumed drink in the world, after water. Around the world, 3 billion cups of tea are drunk every day, made from 1.4 million kilos of tea.

Although we drink many different varieties of tea – from English breakfast to Japanese sencha and hundreds more – all tea leaves originate from the same plant, *Camellia sinensis*.

Camellia sinensis is an evergreen shrub or small tree that is cultivated in tropical and sub-tropical regions across the world. Tea leaves burst with flavour only if they grow in wet, temperate climates that have sunny days alternating with rain-filled nights and cool breezes. Left to grow naturally, a tea tree can reach a height of 3 metres right up to 20 metres, but for cultivation it is usually trimmed to below 2 metres. The leaves can be 4–15 centimetres long and 2–3 centimetres wide.

Tea trees can lead productive lives for up to 150 years. Many of the most famous tea plantations around the world now have trees that are at the end of their working lives and tea planters have been replenishing their plantations and saving time by buying trees grown from cuttings. Unfortunately, these are not as hardy as trees grown from seed. Trees cultivated from cuttings are viable for about 40 years and their shallow roots degrade the soil more quickly by draining it of minerals. Because of this, many tea planters have reverted to growing trees from seed.

Once the tree is ready to be harvested, growers must be careful not to over-pick it, as this can endanger the tree's health. You need to have a lot of patience to produce a good crop of tea leaves!

When tea is harvested the pickers take only the top bud, together with one, two or three leaves below it. It is the way the picked leaves are processed that determines the final type of tea, whether black, green or white.

The flavour and aroma of the leaves depends on the degree of enzymatic oxidation they have undergone. For tea processors, making tea from the leaves of *Camellia sinensis* is like turning grapes into wine – it takes knowledge and talent.

When the cell walls of a tea leaf are broken, the enzymes or proteins within the cell react with oxygen to change the colour and taste of the leaf. This is oxidation, and is the method tea producers use to convert the leaf into different types of tea: oolong, green, black and so on.

Opposite page
The beautiful leaf of the *Camellia sinensis* bush.

This method was discovered thousands of years ago when tea growers first started to put freshly picked leaves into boiled water. However, as fresh tea leaves spoil very quickly, the growers tried preserving them by laying them out in the sun to dry. The heat of the sun on the leaves created oxidation, the leaf changed and processed tea was born.

These days, tea is sent straight to the processing plant after harvesting and for this reason most tea plantations have their own processing plants on site.

Tea processing

Tea leaves go through various processing stages. Firstly, the leaves are softened by a 'withering' process, which reduces the moisture by half and enables them to be rolled without breaking. This is done by laying out the picked leaves in troughs that have air pumped through side vents. This process can take up to 17 hours and the leaves have a wilted appearance at the end.

Next, the leaves are rolled to break down cell walls, promote oxidation and release essential oils. There are two types of rolling: the orthodox rolling, where the leaves are fed onto a belt and gently broken by the rollers, and CTC (cut, tear, curl), where a machine cuts and tears the leaves into smaller pieces.

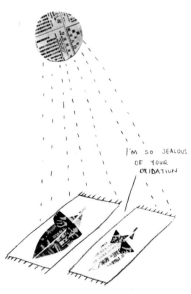

I'M SO JEALOUS OF YOUR OXIDATION

In orthodox rolling, the piles of leaves are held in copper vats and rolled into a compact mass for 10–20 minutes. Next, differing levels of pressure are applied to the leaves to release the oils. If the rolling is too intense, the leaves will be the wrong colour and dull, and if it is too light, then the leaves will be dry and dusty, producing a thin, tasteless liquid.

The rolled leaves are placed on long mats to be sorted according to size and condition, and then laid out to oxidise, or ferment. This process, which can last up to 2 hours, will affect the overall taste and quality of the tea. Fermentation is created by keeping the leaves in an environment with a strictly controlled temperature – from 22–28 degrees Celsius – and humidity levels of at least 90 per cent. Maintaining these levels is crucial because a small rise in temperature will give the tea a burnt taste, while fermentation will stop if the temperature drops even slightly.

If these levels are maintained, the leaf goes through several chemical reactions, heating up and then cooling off. The tea processor's job is a tricky one, as the best results are obtained when fermentation is halted just as the leaf stops heating, which can take from 1–3 hours. Many factory managers say that the best time to stop fermenting the leaves is when they start to smell of apples!

The fascinating thing about fermentation is that although we know all about the flavours that are produced, we don't know a lot about how they are produced. Even tea experts admit that while we understand that certain cellular reactions take place during fermentation, we don't fully comprehend them.

The final stage of processing tea is drying the leaves. This halts the process of oxidation by changing the enzymes that cause it. Once the leaves have

Opposite page
Hand-crafted tea is mainly from China, where it is hand rolled or bundled, and curled into tiny pieces of art.

cooled down, the final stage is placing the fermented leaves in large machines that are placed on conveyor belts that carry them through large dryers. This exposes them to temperatures of around 79 degrees Celsius for approximately 20 minutes. Timing is again of the essence, as too little drying could lead to mouldy leaves and too much erodes the tea's flavour. Drying the leaves reduces the moisture content of the leaves to between 2–6 per cent.

After this stage, the tea is sorted into grades, which is done by putting the leaves into large sieves of varying sizes that are placed on top of each other. As each one vibrates, the tea falls through the holes, with the largest leaves remaining on top and the crushed leaves or 'fannings' falling through to be gathered below.

Where is tea grown?

The tea tree has been growing wild in Xishuangbanna, in the Chinese province of Yunnan, for about 4000 years. However, tea plantations were reported in China from the beginning of the fourth century.

China

China produces mainly green tea. In Chinese plantations, freshly picked tea leaves are steamed for less than a minute in large vats to kill the fermentation enzymes that would otherwise spoil the taste. Next, they are kneaded by hand, put in small piles and regularly turned during a 10-hour drying period. The tea is then rolled according to its grade and sorted. Gunpowder tea is the name for the tiny balls, from one to three millimetres in diameter, used for mint tea in North Africa and Asia. Chun-mee tea has rolled leaves one centimetre long and sencha tea has whole, unrolled leaves. Matcha tea is the powdered tea used for *chanoyu*, the Japanese tea ceremony.

A tea called Yin Zhen (Silver Needles) is produced in Fujian province. In the past, young virgins in gloves, using gold scissors, clipped only the bud and first leaf from the bush, placing them in a golden basket. Nowadays, the tea is plucked on only two days of the year and if the weather conditions are not absolutely ideal, the harvest is cancelled.

India

Most of the tea in India is grown in the northern regions of Darjeeling and Assam. Darjeeling's gardens, high up in the mountains between Nepal and Bhutan, produce the rarest and most valuable black teas. The varying taste of Darjeeling teas are due to differences in altitude, wind and rainfall and they also change according to the seasons. Tea tasters can distinguish between a 'first flush' tea harvested in spring, a 'second flush' tea harvested in early summer and an autumn tea.

In Assam the climate is much hotter and wetter, making it a natural greenhouse. The teas produced in this region are known for having a strong, malty taste and a dark colour, making them an ideal morning tea.

Opposite page
Tea is grown in some of the world's most beautiful and exotic locations. The production processes, from picking to rolling, are mostly manual and require great skill.

SIR THOMAS LIPTON!

Sri Lanka

With a favourable climate that allows for several harvests a year, the island formerly known as Ceylon produces some of the most famous teas in the world. However, its tea industry is a relatively new one. Before 1860, the island was covered with coffee plantations. In that year, a Scottish coffee grower called James Taylor obtained a few tea-tree seeds and tried to grow them. This would have remained an eccentric hobby if it hadn't been for the arrival of a parasitic fungus in 1869, which wiped out all the coffee plants. Growers, looking for an alternative crop, asked Taylor for cuttings from his trees and the tea industry was born. By 1872, the Ceylonese had started to export tea, mainly to England. General merchant Thomas Lipton arrived on the island in 1890, buying up tea plantations and investing in processing machinery.

An early morning tea tasting of the previous day's harvest in Sri Lanka.

Taiwan

The island of Taiwan, formerly known as Formosa, produces superb-quality tea. Its climate is ideal for tea-growing – the temperature stays within a range of 13 to 28 degrees Celsius and humidity is high. As a result of this, Taiwan's tea harvest is a long one, lasting from April to November. The island's speciality is oolong tea and drinking its best-quality tea, Ti Kuan Yin (the Goddess), is said to eliminate all impurities from the body.

Taiwan has a fascinating history; during the sixteenth and seventeenth centuries it was occupied successively by the Portuguese, Spanish, Dutch and English. The Dutch were the first ones to develop the tea trade, but it was Englishman John Dodd who offered credit to plantation owners and also helped to build processing factories in the late 1860s. Today, Taiwanese tea is highly prized.

Japan

Tea was introduced to Japan in the ninth century by a Buddhist monk called Saicho, who had travelled to China to study Buddhism. The monks used tea to stay awake during their long hours of meditation. By the twelfth century, a travelling monk called Eisai had brought a Chinese method of tea preparation back to Japan that involved grinding the tea leaves to a fine powder (matcha) before being brewed.

Japan only produces green tea, known as ocha. The finest ocha, called Gyokuro (Precious Dew), is grown near Kyoto. When the first buds appear, the whole plantation is covered with mats to filter out most of the light. The tiny leaves that grow in the half-light have a higher chlorophyll content, turning them bright green, and they also have a smoother, more mellow flavour due to the lower tannin content.

After the leaves are processed, tea samples are sorted and graded.

Africa

Many African countries started cultivating tea in the nineteenth century as a direct result of being colonised by European countries, which had developed a taste for drinking black tea.

The first tea gardens were planted in South Africa in the 1850s and today more than ten African countries produce tea, although the highest-quality tea can be found in Kenya and Malawi. African tea plantations process mainly black tea and are famous for their high-yield output. Kenya and Malawi have also greatly improved their processing methods and have even started to produce white and green teas. In fact, Kenya now produces so much tea that it is the third-largest tea grower in the world.

Most of the trees in Malawi are *assamica* variety, imported from India as they are best suited to the sub-tropical climate. Malawan teas are still relatively unknown in the West and are usually used in tea blends. ◾

From picking to sipping

All tea comes from the same bush, of which there are two varieties: *Camellia sinensis* and *Camellia assamica. Camellia sinensis,* native to southeastern Asia, is usually used for white, green, oolong and some black tea, while the *assamica* variety, native to India's Assam region, is normally used for black tea. It is the way the leaves are processed that gives us the hundreds of varieties of tea.

1 Picking

The process of picking the tea leaves from the shrub is very specific. Teas are classified according to the time of year they are picked, what part of the tea bud or leaf is picked and where the plants are grown. White teas, for example, are picked only once a year in spring when the new-growth tea buds emerge.

4 Oxidation

The rolled or broken leaves are now laid out in a cool, humid atmosphere for a period that varies according to the type of tea being made. The broken cells absorb oxygen, which brings about chemical changes in the leaf. This is a critical stage in the production process – oxidation is a delicate art that has great influence on how the finished tea will taste. A matter of minutes can cause dramatic differences in flavour and aroma.

2 Withering

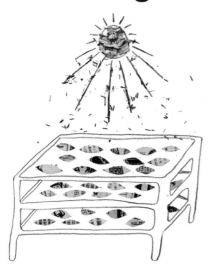

The picked leaves are laid out on a flat surface to wither. This causes the leaves to become limp and flexible so that they can be twisted without cracking or splitting the surface of the leaf. During this process the leaves emit an aroma similar to grated green apple.

3 Rolling

The withered leaves are rolled, twisted or rubbed by machine or hand. This breaks the cells in the leaf and releases the enzymes critical to the oxidation process. When it is done after drying (the last step in the process), it allows the leaf to be transformed into an attractive or a characteristic shape.

5 Drying, frying, steaming

Most teas are dried mechanically, but some are pan-fried by hand, steamed or sun-dried. This stage stops the oxidation process by applying heat, which deactivates the oxidising enzymes and eliminates any moisture remaining in the leaf. The application of heat also expels any grassy odours and locks in the more refined aromas of the tea leaves.

T2 tea lingo

Liquor
Definition Brewed tea (liquid). We often comment on the colour of the liquor of a tea (rich orange, red hues, and so on).

Aroma
Definition The scent of the brewed tea and its leaves.
E.g. a strong aroma.

Notes
Definition The distinct flavours or scents in a tea.
E.g. A complex tisane with notes of cinnamon and ginger.

Finish
Definition How the taste of the tea 'finishes' on your taste buds.
E.g. A subtle brew with a light, savoury finish.

Mouthfeel
Definition The feeling of the tea in your mouth. Is it astringent (black or green tea) or does it feel creamy/buttery (oolong)?

Lingers
Definition A taste that remains after you have swallowed the tea.

Wet leaf
Definition Brewed tea leaves.

Dry leaf
Definition Unbrewed tea leaves.

Steeped
Definition Brewed tea.

All for the love of tea

Use our tea tasting wheel to find the words that best describe the taste of your brew.

Big world of Tea

At **T2**, we group our teas according to type: black, green, herbal infusions, and so on. Here are our main categories, and how best to enjoy them.

White tea

Of all the tea varieties in all the lands, white teas are the most revered. Offering a restrained palate of multilayered light, tender, sweet and ethereal flavours, white tea makes a fascinatingly complex drink. With just a touch of caffeine, it is also the least processed of all, and thus the closest tea comes to its natural state.

White teas are traditionally produced from the new-season's spring harvest, which lasts for two weeks. They are highly prized due to their rarity: in ancient China, they were reserved exclusively for emperors and other high-ranking officials.

The name comes from the fine silvery-white hairs on the unopened buds of the tea plant that give it a whitish appearance. White teas are usually divided into two types; those made only from the downy buds and those made from the bud and first leaf from the new season's tea bush.

The tea undergoes very little processing; once picked it is simply withered and dried. During the withering phase, the leaves are spread out over bamboo racks and, depending on the weather, left to air-dry for 12–24 hours. Sometimes fans of different intensities are used to increase air circulation.

Traditionally, the leaves are not fired, so that their pale colour and delicate flavour are preserved. White tea leaves produce a very subtle-tasting liquid, said by its devotees to be exceptionally refreshing. ▪

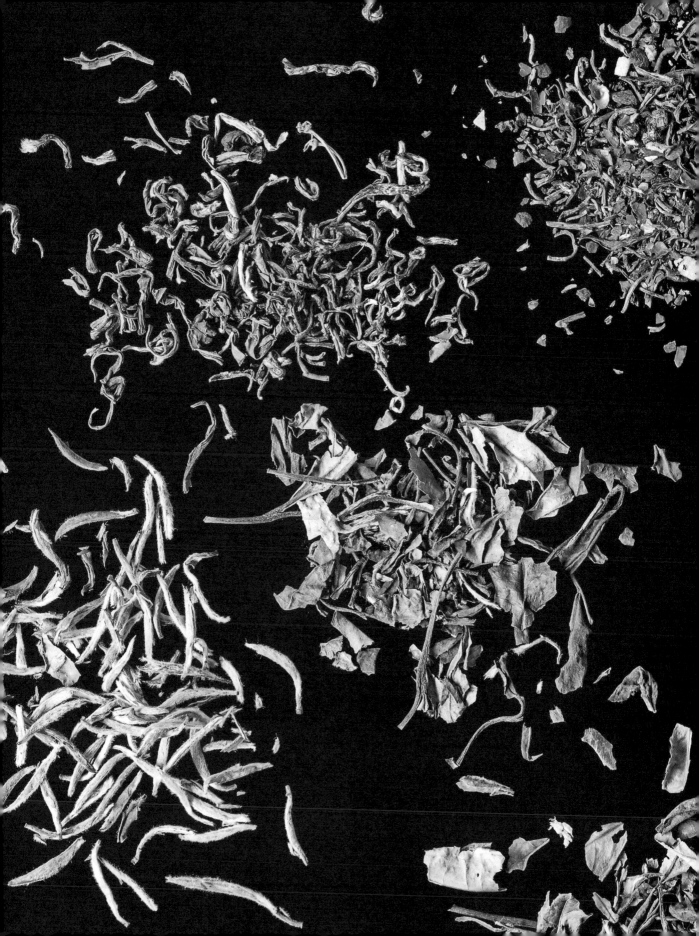

Yellow tea

The sweet, loveable twin sister of green tea, yellow tea is subtle and mild, and has the characteristics of green tea without its sometimes bitter, grassy undertones. Antioxidant-rich, yellow tea is prized for its fresh and flowery aromas.

Although they have been in existence for several hundred years, yellow teas are becoming increasingly rare – the process for making yellow tea is a time-consuming and difficult one. While we have a thousand kinds of green tea, there are only a handful of yellow teas that survive today.

To get a high-quality yellow, only the bud is picked, before it becomes downy. One Chinese province, Hunan, still produces limited quantities, ensuring the survival of this prestigious tea.

It is called 'yellow' because of the way it is processed. After being dehydrated, the warm leaves are spread out on the ground and covered with a damp cloth for a period of 4–10 hours.

Covering the leaves raises their temperature, which triggers a slight oxidation by creating steam. This process gives the leaves a yellowish tinge. The resulting tea liquor generally has a very yellow-green appearance and smells quite different from white tea and green tea. ◻

Green tea

Green tea was first produced in China, but its popularity has spread to most of the countries of Asia, and in particular Japan. There are more than 1500 varieties of green tea, many of which can be both calming and reviving. Getting the brewing time right is essential for all teas, but especially with this very complex variety.

The leaves are picked when young, just the bud plus one or two leaves. Depending on the processor, the leaves may or may not be dried or 'withered'. In order to halt the oxidation process, the tea is then either steamed or pan-fried, which preserves the green colour.

The leaves are rolled into a twisted, flat needle or bead shape and then dried in order to stabilise the aromatic oils and remove any remaining water. This also reduces the risk of mould. Finally, they are sifted through a fine sieve to get rid of any broken leaves. With the exception of matcha, a powdered green tea produced in Japan, unfermented teas are always whole-leaf teas.

Green tea is judged on its aroma and on the length of its flavour. Westerners often find green tea to be bitter, but this can be eliminated by rinsing the tea leaves in water before placing in the pot. High-quality green teas are said to fill the palate with a lasting, aromatic, slightly sweet flavour.

These teas are absolutely delicious just as they are; there is no need for milk or sugar. ◻

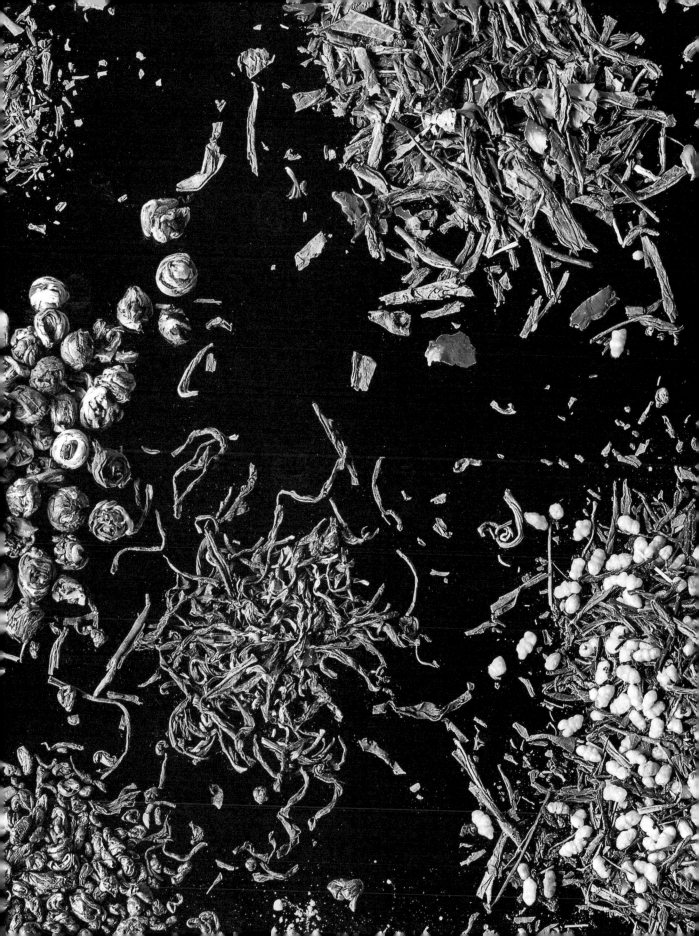

Oolong tea

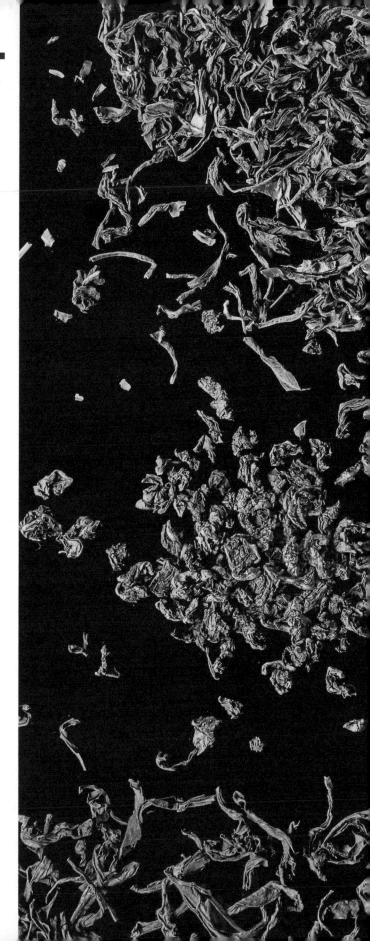

When you make a cup of oolong tea, the khaki green leaves expand upon brewing to produce a light, clear, yellow infusion. Ooolong tea makes a well-balanced brew with a delightfully nutty aroma. A smooth resinous taste transforms into nutty, woody flavours with a hint of smoke. Oolong tea is said to have a calming effect on the body.

Oolong tea is a semi-fermented tea, and is very popular in China and Taiwan. Oolong teas taste smoother than black tea and less grassy than green tea.

An oolong tea can be closer to a green or a black tea depending on the oxidation. Green oolong teas have undergone 30–50 per cent oxidation and black oolong teas can be up to 70 per cent oxidised. Green oolong teas have a vegetal or floral bouquet, while black oolong teas smell sweeter and woodier.

Good-quality oolong tea can be steeped a few times from the same leaves. Unlike other types of tea, it actually improves with re-brewing and it is often said that the third or fourth steeping is the best.

For the oxidation process, the withered leaves are spread out on bamboo trays in a room with a controlled temperature and humidity, and stirred regularly. During the stirring, the friction of the leaves against the bamboo trays releases aromatic oils, triggering the oxidation process. During this time, the growers constantly touch and sniff the leaves, using their senses to determine if the tea is ready. ▦

Black tea

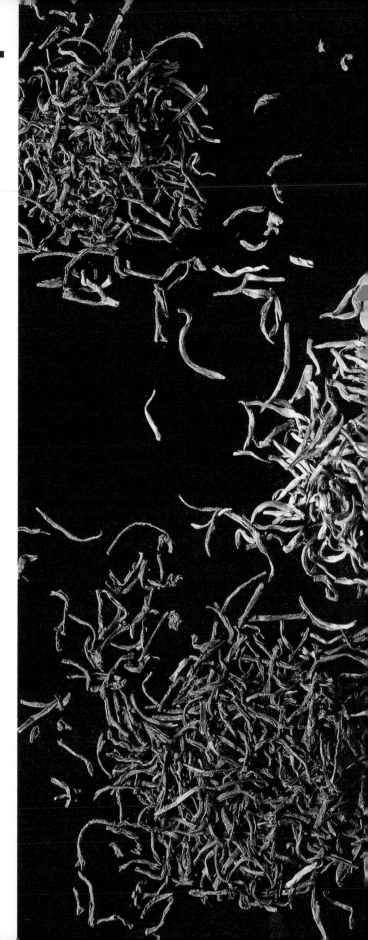

Arguably the world's most popular drink, black tea is more assertive than green or oolong teas, but nevertheless has subtle complexities that make it enduringly popular. Black tea contains higher levels of caffeine than its counterparts and is rich in antioxidants. In China, black teas are called 'red teas' due to the copper colour of the infusion.

Black tea's strong flavour and heady aromas mean that it can be enjoyed with milk and sugar, and it has earned its place as the variety of choice for many Western tea drinkers.

Black tea is made from fully oxidised tea leaves, which go through four main stages of processing.

First, the leaves are laid in vented troughs and air is pumped through to remove the moisture in the leaves. This gives them a wilted appearance.

Then, the leaves are rolled or cut and torn by special machines, which breaks down the cell walls and releases the essential oils in the leaves.

The rolled leaves are then sorted by size and condition and laid out to oxidise, or ferment. Fermentation is created by keeping the leaves in a controlled temperature of 22–27 degrees Celsius, with at least 90 per cent humidity.

In the final stage, the leaves are exposed to a heat of at least 80 degrees Celsius for 20 minutes to dry them. The dried tea can then be sorted into grades. ◼

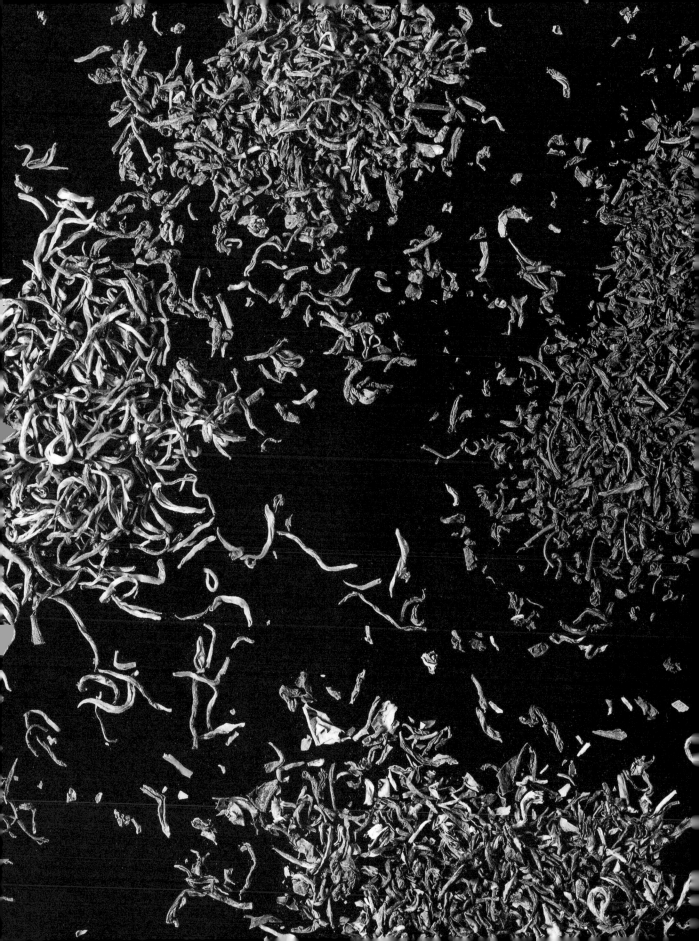

Flavoured tea

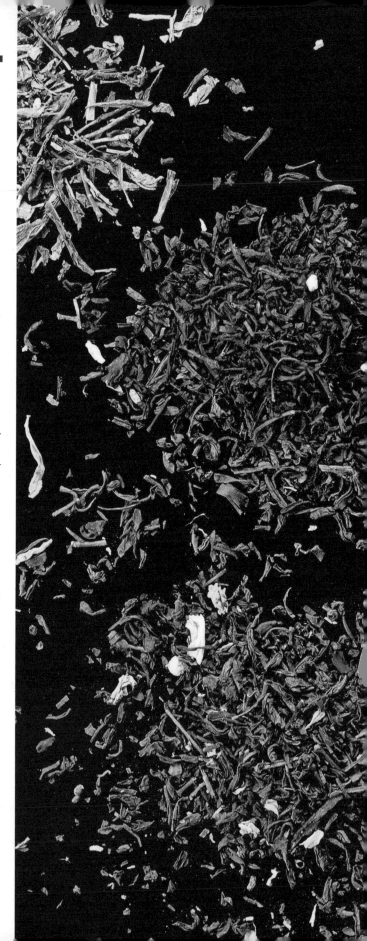

If you are taking your first steps into the world of tea drinking, flavoured teas are an easy place to start. Black tea is usually used as a base, and every type of fruit, spices like cinnamon and cloves, and oils and essences from nuts, herbs and flowers can be added to it for a delicious flavour hit.

Another way to flavour tea is to add various flavourings. We use nature-identical flavours, which are the same as those found in nature but more potent. These fragrant liquids are misted onto the teas as they are rotated in a vast tumbler.

Whether you feel like a light, sweet and fruity infusion, or a luscious caramel/chocolate dessert-like drop, there is a flavoured tea that will hit the spot. Several flavoured teas had noble beginnings, including Earl Grey and chai.

Earl Grey

Earl Grey tea is named after Lord Grey, who was prime minister of Britain in the 1830s. One day he received a gift from China of some tea flavoured with oil of bergamot, a small citrus tree. He loved it and ordered more. Today, it is one of the most popular tea blends in the world.

Chai

The invention of chai goes back thousands of years in India. It is said to have been created as a healing brew used in the healing tradition of Ayurvedic medicine. In ancient times it was thought that chai could naturally heal the body and soul. Today, however, our chai teas are a rich, sensory blend of exotic herbs and spices, which in the depths of winter can warm the soul from the first sip. ◼

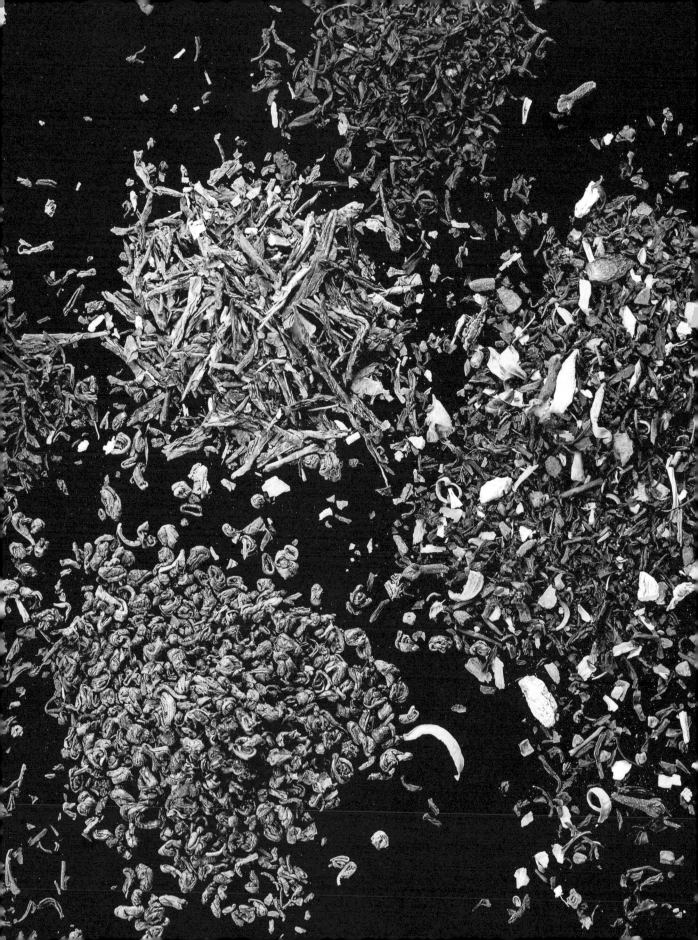

Hand-crafted tea

Hand-crafted teas are almost always Chinese – well, at T2 they are. Blooming tea or flowering tea is another name for this type of tea. You would have seen these beautiful bundles of tea in restaurants or gift stores, where dried tea leaves are bundled together and wrapped around flowers, then set aside to dry. Once popped into hot water, these brilliant balls unfurl slowly to release the flower within – it's a very theatrical tea-drinking experience.

There are hundreds of teas in this category – they come in the most amazing shapes and sizes, and the tastes and aromas are exciting and always different. All of these teas are processed and handmade by skilled artisans.

One of our favourite versions of hand-crafted tea is called Buddha's Tears. Green tea leaves are used, a jasmine leaf is wrapped into the fold and they are rolled into what looks like a little tea pearl. Once these are put into boiling water they unravel spectacularly to release a beautiful jasmine aroma and taste – a delicate tea-drinking delight.

Mudan Rose is also a classic hand-crafted tea. On one of my recent trips I even came across tea flowers dusted in silver and gold leaf, which is certainly taking things to a new level!

We suggest you use a glass teapot or glass cups for brewing hand-crafted tea, as is it such a beautiful thing to watch – it would be a waste to brew it in anything else. ▦

Rooibos

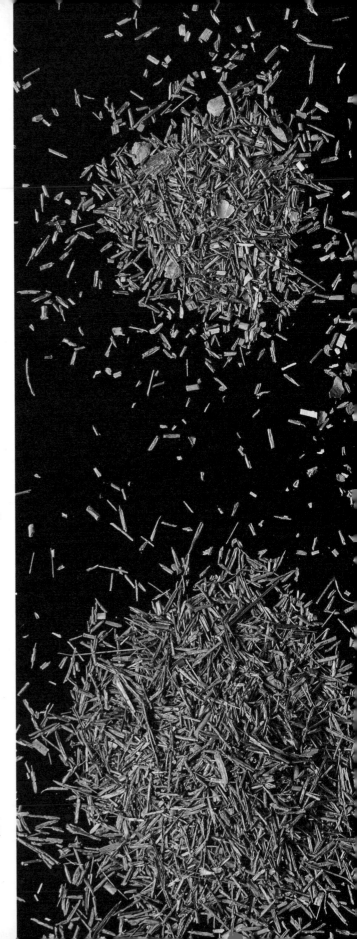

Though not technically 'tea', rooibos or 'red bush' is brewed to make a tea-like beverage that is now widely enjoyed across the globe.

This African bush tea, cultivated from a shrub native to South Africa, was first drunk by Dutch settlers as a cheaper alternative to black tea, which had to come on supply ships all the way from Europe and so was prohibitively expensive.

Rooibos is caffeine-free and high in antioxidants and minerals. Now recognised for its health benefits – it is said to improve circulation, relieve stomach complaints, reduce the effect of skin conditions and encourage a restful sleep – it is growing in popularity.

The rooibos bush grows to 1–2 metres in height and is covered with small branches. The leaves and stems are harvested and then cut, crushed, oxidised and dried in the sun. Rooibos tea has a fruity, slightly sweet, mellow flavour with acidic overtones.

Unoxidised or 'green' rooibos is also produced, but the more demanding production process (similar to the method for producing green tea) makes it more expensive than traditional rooibos. It has a malty and slightly grassy flavour, quite different to its red sibling.

In South Africa, it is common to prepare rooibos tea in the same way as black tea and add milk and sugar to taste. Otherwise, you can add a slice of lemon and use honey instead of sugar. ■

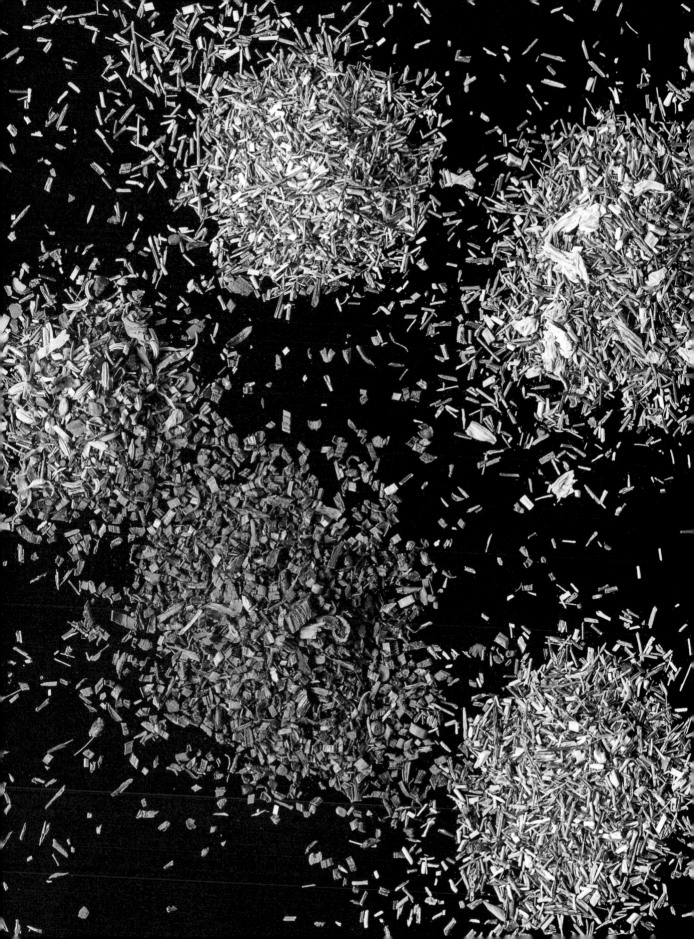

Fruit and herbal tisanes

Fruit tisanes are the sweethearts of the tea world. You can drink them year-round. They are perfect as a hot brew, especially if you are at the snowfields and you want a fruity, cinnamon sip to warm your soul after a hard day's skiing.

At T2, however, drinking fruit tisanes is often an iced experience as they lend themselves beautifully to chilling, are deliciously refreshing, and you can really enjoy the beautiful colours they create.

These fruity drinks, which are also called infusions, are made from the leaves and flowers of fruits. Fruit tisanes also look beautiful in the container – they are the prettiest of teas, and we carefully choose the ingredients for their beauty, flavour and compatibility.

Some fruit teas are best for a boost, some after a meal, others to calm you at the end of the day. Whatever the reason for your brew, you can enjoy all sorts of combinations – just let your imagination and your palate be your guide.

You can also use fruit teas to sweeten other teas, as there is a lot of naturally occurring sweetness in them.

Fruit blends are perfect for something naturally sweet in the fridge at all times or for a delicious surprise in school drink bottles.

Smoked and scented tea

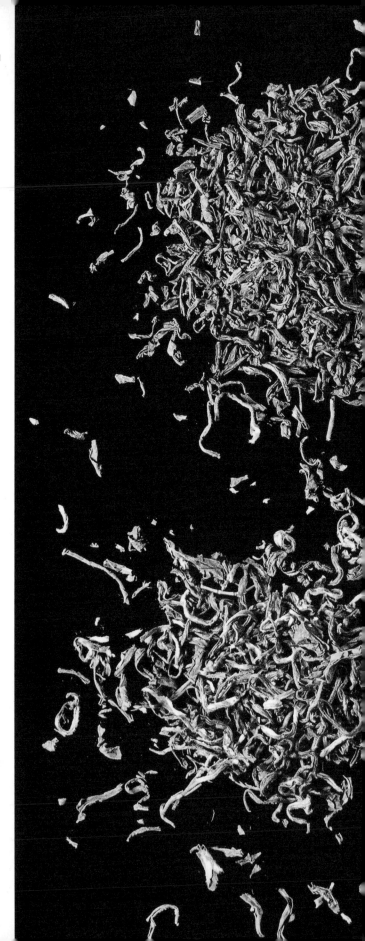

Smoked teas

Legend has it that, in the early nineteenth century, a Chinese tea grower was forced to hand over his plantation to the government. Reluctant to relinquish his harvest, he quickly dried it by placing the leaves over a fire of burning pine roots, which gave the tea a distinctive smoky aroma. The leaves were exported to Europe, where they were instantly popular.

Smoked teas, or lapsang souchong, are produced from teas called su-chong, which are dried over burning pine branches, giving them a characteristic resin aroma and taste.

Nowadays, the tea leaves undergo a complex smoking process that results in a distinctive aroma of woody pine smoke and tobacco notes. Long, lingering smokiness defines this memorable brew, and it also has a definite caffeine kick.

If you like single malt whiskies, you will love smoked tea.

Scented teas

Scenting tea is one of the oldest ways to add flavour to a tea. The tea is most commonly scented with jasmine blossom or rose petals and buds. The tea is laid out and then covered in a layer of blossoms. Layer upon layer is created like this, sometimes up to eight layers deep. This is done at night, when the blossoms release their strongest scent. Once the tea has absorbed the scent, the jasmine or rose blossoms are discarded.

Tea will absorb any flavour that is placed next to it, which is why it is important to store it in an airtight container. ■

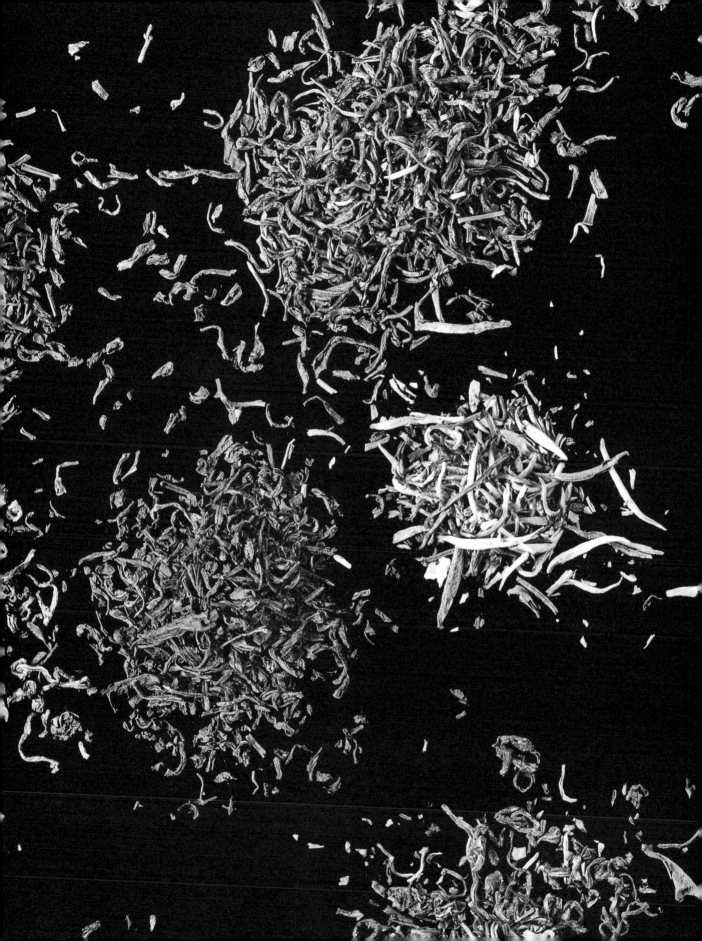

Perfect brewing

	3-7 mins	1-3 mins	1-3 mins	3-6 mins

100°C

90°C

80°C

White Tea Yellow Tea Green Tea Oolong Tea

Do you like your tea strong or light, smoky or sweet? You need to know these preferences before you commence the three steps of perfect brewing.

The first step is selecting the right leaf, one to suit your mood. If you want a strong brew, make sure you've selected a leaf that is mostly broken or open, because it will brew up stronger and quicker. If you feel like a light tea, choose a mostly whole leaf, as it will give you a lighter brew. The diagrams on the following pages explain why the brewing time varies according to different types of leaves.

The three most important things when brewing a perfect cup of tea are:
1. Leaf selection
2. Water temperature
3. Timing – how long you infuse

If you will be adding milk to black tea, add another minute of brewing time – this will ensure that lovely honey colour and strength of flavour to complement the milk.

 Boiling water

Cold or tap water

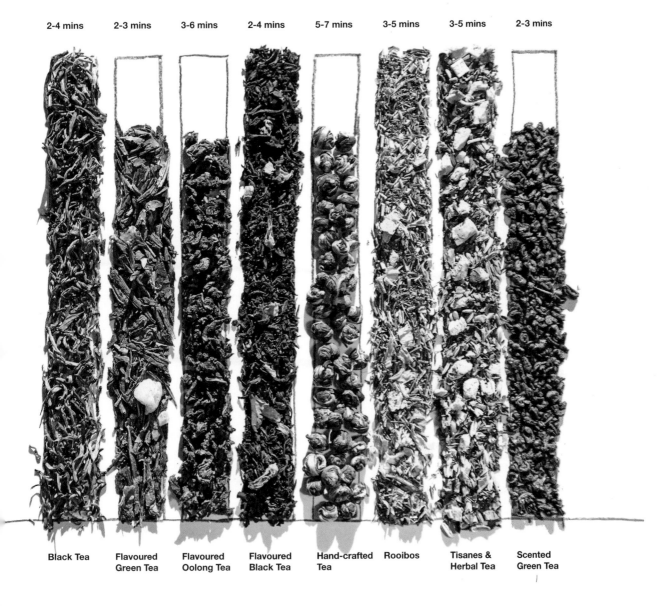

2-4 mins	2-3 mins	3-6 mins	2-4 mins	5-7 mins	3-5 mins	3-5 mins	2-3 mins
Black Tea	Flavoured Green Tea	Flavoured Oolong Tea	Flavoured Black Tea	Hand-crafted Tea	Rooibos	Tisanes & Herbal Tea	Scented Green Tea

80°C

To achieve a lower temperature, fill your pot with one-fifth cold or tap water and four-fifths boiling water, then add your infuser. Don't pour boiling water directly over some of the lighter teas, like most white and green teas.

100°C

Certain teas need to be brewed at 100°C. That's why we recommend heating your teapot with hot or boiling water before adding the water you'll use to brew your tea. Otherwise, the water will cool before you start brewing.

White tea

mins

0

1

2

3

4

5

6

7

Pai Mu Tan
Open tea leaves brew more quickly than just the buds.

Silver Needles
Delicate buds take longer to allow all the flavour to be released.

Yellow tea

mins

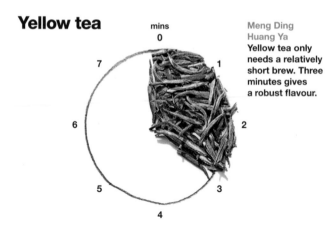

0

1

2

3

4

5

6

7

Meng Ding Huang Ya
Yellow tea only needs a relatively short brew. Three minutes gives a robust flavour.

Green tea

mins

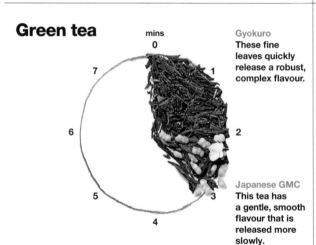

0

1

2

3

4

5

6

7

Gyokuro
These fine leaves quickly release a robust, complex flavour.

Japanese GMC
This tea has a gentle, smooth flavour that is released more slowly.

Oolong tea

mins

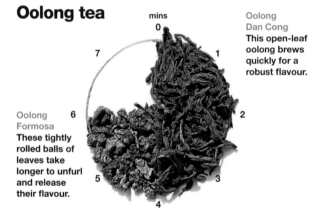

0

1

2

3

4

5

6

7

Oolong Dan Cong
This open-leaf oolong brews quickly for a robust flavour.

Oolong Formosa
These tightly rolled balls of leaves take longer to unfurl and release their flavour.

Black tea

mins

0

1

2

3

4

5

6

7

English Breakfast
This broken-leaf tea brews quickly and has a robust flavour.

Grand Yunnan
This tea is mainly made up of buds, so it brews more slowly to reveal a mellow, complex flavour.

Flavoured green tea

mins

0

1

2

3

4

5

6

7

Gorgeous Geisha
A quick brew is all that's needed to release the sencha and strawberry flavours.

Sencha Vanilla
The smooth vanilla flavours work well with a longer brew.

Flavoured oolong tea

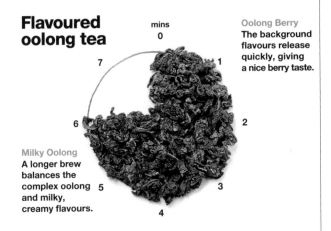

mins
0

7
1
6
2
5
3
4

Oolong Berry
The background flavours release quickly, giving a nice berry taste.

Milky Oolong
A longer brew balances the complex oolong and milky, creamy flavours.

Flavoured black tea

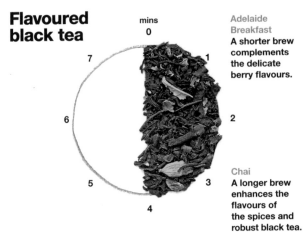

mins
0

7
1
6
2
5
3
4

Adelaide Breakfast
A shorter brew complements the delicate berry flavours.

Chai
A longer brew enhances the flavours of the spices and robust black tea.

Hand-crafted tea

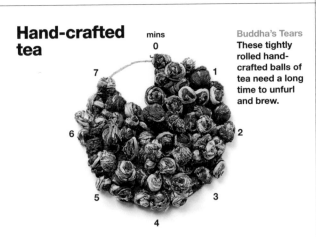

mins
0

7
1
6
2
5
3
4

Buddha's Tears
These tightly rolled hand-crafted balls of tea need a long time to unfurl and brew.

Rooibos

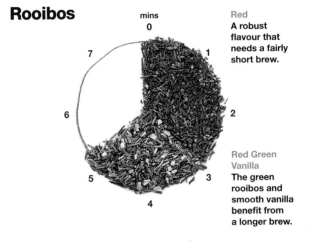

mins
0

7
1
6
2
5
3
4

Red
A robust flavour that needs a fairly short brew.

Red Green Vanilla
The green rooibos and smooth vanilla benefit from a longer brew.

Tisanes and herbal tea

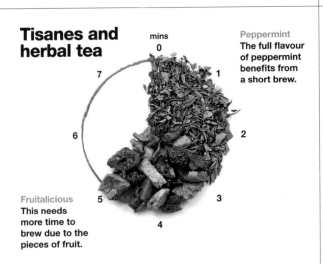

mins
0

7
1
6
2
5
3
4

Peppermint
The full flavour of peppermint benefits from a short brew.

Fruitalicious
This needs more time to brew due to the pieces of fruit.

Scented green tea

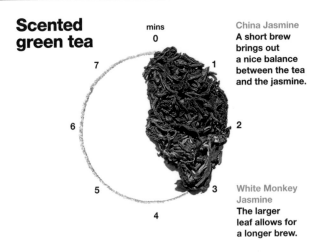

mins
0

7
1
6
2
5
3
4

China Jasmine
A short brew brings out a nice balance between the tea and the jasmine.

White Monkey Jasmine
The larger leaf allows for a longer brew.

The perfect cup of tea

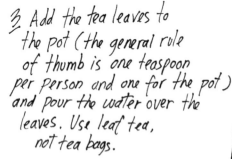

1 Boil water in a kettle—make sure it is fresh water every time and never use a microwave to heat your water.

2 Pour a little of the boiling water into your teapot to warm it up, then discard.

3 Add the tea leaves to the pot (the general rule of thumb is one teaspoon per person and one for the pot) and pour the water over the leaves. Use leaf tea, not tea bags.

4 Add just-boiled water for black tea, but for green or white tea, the optimum temperature is as low as 80°C.

T2

FULL-BODIED
BLACK TEA

TASTING THE

TASTE OF HOT

PANCAKES

T2™
NEW YORK
BREAKFAST

5. Let the tea brew for a few minutes (see pages 60-61 for brewing instructions)

6. Find out who prefers strong or weak tea, and pour the tea accordingly (weak cups first).

7. Add the milk, if desired — enough to make a reddish-brown colour, or to your liking.

Milk

When adding milk to tea you need to be very careful that you select a robust tea that produces a great dark brew. These teas can cope with the colour of milk and, of course, its richness. Assam, English or Irish Breakfast tea are the best teas to serve with milk.

Assam will give you a beautiful red/biscuity coloured tea, and it also handles a touch of sweetness perfectly.

Most Sri Lankan teas will take milk well, as will a small selection of flavoured teas such as T2's Chocolate or Terrific Toffee, because their underlying flavour is rich and warming.

Never add milk to any Chinese or Darjeeling teas.

Do you take your tea with milk?

- Choose a robust, full-flavoured black tea.
- You need to brew your tea to full strength without over-brewing – say 4 minutes for Assam or the Breakfast teas, then add milk.
- I personally never add the milk before the tea. I believe you should add your milk to the point where the colour is to your liking, and this will vary every time.
- Full-cream cows' milk will give you the most traditional flavour and the best colour.
- The best T2 tea for a milky brew is Chai. Chai is an Indian spice/herbal blended tea that is served with milk almost all the time and served in India by people known as chai wallahs.
- Chai is traditionally served in terracotta cups that you smash to the ground once you have finished your tea.
- Builder's tea is a colloquial term for tea that is brewed strong (often with a teabag directly in a mug) and served with milk and several spoonfuls of sugar.
- It is common to use alternatives such as soy or almond milk for Chai, but it is our recommendation to stick with full-cream cows' milk for full-bodied tea.

Sugar

Adding sugar to tea is a practice that many people find hard to give up, but be aware that sugar often destroys the flavour of more delicate teas. If you have gone to the effort of selecting a beautiful single-estate tea, such as Darjeeling First Flush, do try to avoid adding sugar as it will camouflage the subtle beauty of the tea.

At T2, we occasionally add honey or other sweeteners to tea, or we will often use our Turkish Apple tisane, which is essentially a sugar-based tea, to sweeten our brews. We also add sweeteners to our herbal tisanes, which don't tend to have the natural sweetness of the fruit tisanes. Many of our fruit tisanes are naturally sweet and are a good way to enjoy a sweet flavour without using sugar.

There is an expectation that iced teas will be sweet. These can be made by using any tea leaf, but the black, green and oolong teas are the ones most likely to need sweetening. If you are using a fruit tisane, you will find these are naturally sweet and shouldn't need extra sweetener. However, you can enhance the sweetness in these brews by adding fresh fruit.

Which teas are best with a little added sweetness?

All breakfast teas

The teas in this category are strong black teas, so they will stand up well to some added sweetness.

Chai

Traditionally, Chai almost always has a dash of honey, and the strength in the ingredients usually demands sweetener of some kind.

Lemongrass and Ginger

At T2, this is a staple and perfect if you are looking to put a bit of pep in your step. Add a touch of honey, or a fruit tea such as Ruby Red Rosehip, and the sweet combination is a delight. ■

Bag vs loose

The best way to make tea is using loose leaf tea, but occasionally a tea bag is the only way. T2 tea bags contain the same tea we sell loose, but just in a bag. The tea you make when using bags will taste different to that made from the loose leaves because the leaves don't have room to dance in your cup or pot while infusing.

T2 directory

T2 offers over 200 teas, give or take, which can be a little overwhelming, so we have come up with a way to give every tea its 15 minutes of fame. As you enter any T2 store the first thing you will come across is our tea table, which holds a bowl of every tea variety we offer in dry leaf. This helps the customer understand the different varieties and helps them define what type of tea drinker they are.

Every six weeks we select up to six teas to sit proudly on our tasting stations, and every day we brew them up in as many ways as we can to show the versatility of the teas and, of course, their taste. More often than not, these are the teas that sell best.

The journey of tea selection is very much part of the complete tea drinking ceremony for our customers, as they will make a very personal choice to suit their likes and dislikes.

White tea

White Rose
Delicate white tea is blended with pretty rose petals for a floral and wonderfully sweet-scented sensation. Preserving the refined nature of the tea, flowers add delicate sweetness that lingers from start to finish.

Pai Mu Tan
This full-bodied bud delights with flowers, honeydew and a hint of chocolate.

Yellow tea

Meng Ding Huang Ya
This rare tea comes from the misty peak of Mount Meng. It is grassy in nature, with a sweet taste and nutty aroma.

Green tea

Gunpowder Green
Tightly rolled balls that are light, a little astringent and very refreshing.

Japanese GMC Sencha
Grassy, delicate and fresh, this gives an instant lift.

Pi Lo Chun
Delicate and highly prized, with hints of chestnuts and a fleeting floral bouquet.

Young Hyson
Medium-bodied and robust with a mellow, sweet finish.

Oolong tea

Oolong Oriental Beauty
This prized oolong is dark and robust, with notes of honey, caramel and fruit.

Ti Kuan Yin
Nutty, fruity flavours balanced with delicate orchids.

Black tea

English Breakfast
A stimulating blend, this classic tea is bright and bitey with a commanding aroma.

Grand Yunnan
A highly-prized complex brew with chocolate and orange aromas and a wisp of smoke.

Lapsang Souchong
A spicy, savoury finish with a long lingering smokiness.

Orange Pekoe
Hints of sugarcane and sultanas, with a light touch of tannins. A clean, brisk finish.

Pu-erh
Revered for its deep, almost coffee-like flavour and complex woody nose.

Flavoured and scented tea

Aussie Wattle Breakfast
Earthy and delightfully nutty, this golden tea is warming, tangy and simply divine.

Banana Bake
Robust black tea with hints of vanilla and banana.

Chai
Our signature blend is spicy, complex and incredibly tasty.

French Earl Grey
Earl Grey with a fruity and floral French twist.

Gorgeous Geisha
Smooth, sweet and delicious. Green tea with the flavour of strawberries and cream.

Green Rose
A sweet, fruity elixir. Elegant sencha and rose enhanced by a blend of tropical fruit.

Melbourne Breakfast
A rich infusion with delicious vanilla and honey notes for a smooth and refreshing brew.

New York Breakfast
A full-bodied black tea boasting the taste of hot pancakes, a brew inspired by a perfect New York moment.

Raspberry Rush
Loads of raspberry flavours and gorgeous red hibiscus petals in a black tea base.

Sencha Sensation
A flavoured green tea with hints of citrus and bergamot for those who like a delicate flavour.

Hand-crafted tea

Buddha's Tears
A sensory treat! Hand-rolled ethereal buds unfurl heavenly, fragrant jasmine flavours.

Chrysanthemum Burst
A glorious bouquet will bloom from hand-crafted, delicate and sweet young pekoe leaves.

Rooibos

Cinnamon Somersault
This tisane is fast-paced and complex, with cinnamon, orange and ginger. You'll be somersaulting in no time.

Honey Honey
An intriguing and aromatic blend of sweet honey, vanilla, candied florals and hot toast.

Tisanes and herbal tea

Apple Crumble
Serve hot or iced. It's good enough to eat.

Bamboo
Deliciously unique, a smooth, honey, sweet pea taste.

Bondi
Picture the colours of this iconic Sydney beach.

Cocoa Loco
This decadent brew will satisfy all your chocolate cravings without the guilt!

Creamy Choc Chai
Super-big, rich chocolatey flavour with a smooth, creamy finish.

Deliciously Dreamy
Dream of sweet tropical evenings.

Fruitalicious
With a tantalising mix of cranberries, blueberries, dragon fruit and goji berries, your taste buds will be screaming for mercy!

Gone Surfing
A herbal and botanical burst of relaxation. Great to calm you down or to get you going.

Indian Spice
A spicy combination of pepper and ginger that will cleanse, warm and invigorate.

Just Chamomile
Refreshing and calming, soothing and sweetly seductive, this is a classy classic to unwind with.

Just Cinnamon
Spice it up with this exotic elixir – it's a sweet, savoury and sultry escape.

Just Peppermint
Minty goodness that is clean, fresh, vibrant and as uplifting as an everglade.

Mint Mix
Peppermint, spearmint and refreshing lemonbalm combine to make a tasty digestive tonic.

Red Fancy Fruit
Rooibos with summer petals and tangy fruit flavours. Smooth and creamy and so hot right now.

Sleep Tight
Say goodnight with this gentle lemony, sweet floral herb blend for dreamy dreams.

Just Ginger
Spicy, fragrant and moreish, this brew delivers Silk Road flavour with a modern twist.

Just Rose
This floral tisane tastes and looks beautiful, and is packed with vitamin C goodness.

Oolong Berry
Raspberries are known as one of the worlds most perfect foods, so we guess that means this tea is in the same prestigious ranks! These beautiful crimson baubles have been combined with a light green oolong tea to create a wonderfully fragrant and intense, yet delicate flavour.

Red Green and Dreamy
Green rooibos with an incredible summer fruity scent of peaches, plums and fresh berries.

Just Hibiscus
Plucked from the heart of the hibiscus flower, this bright tisane is as delicious as it is versatile. The Jamaicans drink hibiscus tea iced and infused with ginger and rum!

Lamington
Sweet chocolate flavours play with hints of coconut on a backdrop of sharp and full-bodied black tea.

Southern Sunrise
White hibiscus, lemongrass and grapefruit bring this fruity brew to life. Designed with an Australian summer in mind, this sunny tisane will brighten any mood or morning. With a tantalising aroma, this tisane can be served hot, or chilled with ice, fresh oranges and lemon slices.

Riotous Rose
Delivering candy-sweet aromas with splashes of rose, strawberries, raspberries and oranges, this floral cuppa is heavenly mouth mayhem and riotously romantic.

Oolong Chocolate Chai
Chocolate, cinnamon, ginger, oolong combination laced with pepper. An intriguing sweet, bright and spicy flavour that will warm you up.

Just Jasmine
A lingering flavour carries you from one sip to the next.

Liquorice Legs
Digestive and cleansing, sweet liquorice blended with peppermint for zap and zing.

Strawberries and Cream
Decadent summer berries blended with velvety yoghurt pieces – a dessert lover's delight!

Ruby Red Rosehip
This rich red blend of rosehips, rose and hibiscus is full of soothing goodness.

Pumping Pomegranate
The essence of the Turkish grand bazaar, this tea will take you on a flavour journey with pumping pomegranate, tangy hibiscus, apple pieces and rosehip along for the ride.

Just Lavender
A light and bright heady floral infusion that is perfect to wind up or to wind down.

Lung Ching Classic
A sought-after Chinese green tea from the Zhejiang province. Bright-green leaves with a nutty, fragrant taste.

Sweet Dreams
Sweet dreams are made of this. Breathe more freely after this tranquil brew, which can wash away even the most chaotic day. Chamomile, apple, silver lime flower and lavender will have you dreaming in no time.

TO
everyone's
cup of tea.

Sip & Slurp

Sip & slurp

I thought I knew a lot about tea before I started T2, but actually I knew very little. The last 18 years have taught me so much about not only the tea leaf, but also about history and about passion, and T2 introduced me to a whole world of tea lovers.

Tea as we know it at T2 is a lifestyle – we don't have a cup of tea, we do tea and it's always a ceremony.

When I decide to brew a pot of tea, I start by thinking about what might suit my mood, or if we have guests, what they might feel like. Then I select the tea-ware to serve it in – that's as important to me as the tea itself.

My teapot collection, as you might imagine, is huge – close to a hundred pots in fact! Each teapot is unique and there is a story that goes with each and every one. My cup, saucer and mug collection is just as diverse, but nothing matches. It's not something I did on purpose, it's just the way it has evolved. This is also something you will see in our store: our collections of tea-wares are eclectic, but they always seem to work together.

Every time someone brews a cup of tea using loose leaf tea it tastes different, because there are so many variables. The taste will depend on the amount of time you allow the tea to brew, the amount of tea leaves you use, the quality of water you use, its temperature, and so on.

The first sip from a fresh cup of tea is a moment's pause in a busy day; you breathe in the aroma as you lift the cup to your lips, you take a slow, gentle sip and wait for the taste to kick in. It's always different, but it's always good. ◼

Matching tea with...

When you select tea, there are lots of factors that come into play, like the time of day, what you are doing or eating, how you are feeling and your personal aesthetics...So we're going to help you choose the right tea for every mood and occasion. Surprise yourself and enjoy!

Food

Pu-erh, Keemun,
Oolong Oriental Beauty, Irish Breakfast
Black teas and dark oolongs are a wonderful balance to full-flavoured meats. The clean, earthy flavour of Pu-erh is fantastic after a heavy meal.

Gyokuro, Dong Ding Oolong,
Oolong Formosa, Grand Yunnan
Whether you're enjoying succulent fresh lobster, delicate sashimi or smoked fish, you'll find a flavour to match here.

Lapsang Souchong, Assam,
Good Afternoon, Keemun
Spicy dishes need a strong tea to stand up and do battle with the spices.

Darjeeling, Lung Ching,
Japanese GMC Sencha, Oolong Dan Cong
A lot of people think of pairing cheese and wine, but the flavours of the cheese can be equally enhanced by tea!

Assam, Ning Hong Jing Hao,
Orange Pekoe, Buddha's Tears
From a hearty rich tea to cut through the sweetness of robust chocolatey desserts to more delicate offerings that are complemented by a sweet jasmine green tea, sweet foods and tea are a historic match.

Lung Ching, Good Evening,
Japanese GMC Sencha, Darjeeling
Most salads will pair really well with a green tea. For salads with strong flavours, try a delicate black tea, like Darjeeling.

Mood

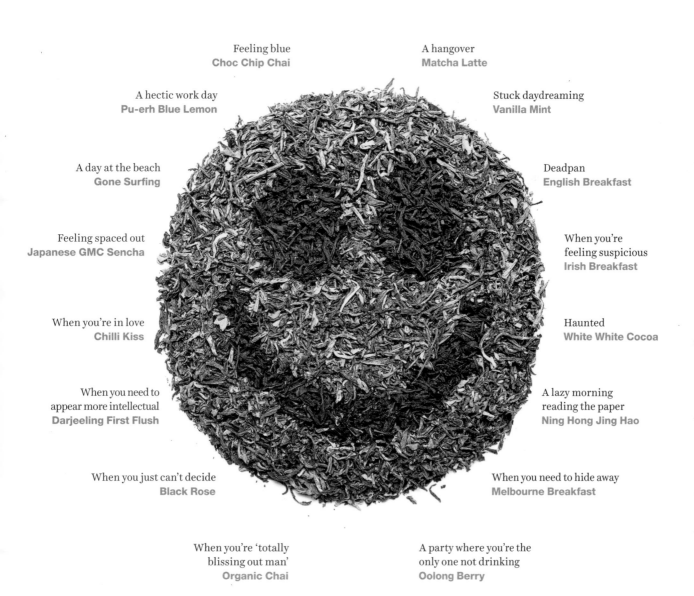

Feeling blue
Choc Chip Chai

A hangover
Matcha Latte

A hectic work day
Pu-erh Blue Lemon

Stuck daydreaming
Vanilla Mint

A day at the beach
Gone Surfing

Deadpan
English Breakfast

Feeling spaced out
Japanese GMC Sencha

When you're
feeling suspicious
Irish Breakfast

When you're in love
Chilli Kiss

Haunted
White White Cocoa

When you need to
appear more intellectual
Darjeeling First Flush

A lazy morning
reading the paper
Ning Hong Jing Hao

When you just can't decide
Black Rose

When you need to hide away
Melbourne Breakfast

When you're 'totally
blissing out man'
Organic Chai

A party where you're the
only one not drinking
Oolong Berry

Late night studying
Matcha

Time of day

Pi Lo Chun

Sleep Tight

Dong Ding Oolong

Lavender Lullaby

Brilliant

Cocoa Loco

Grand Yunnan

Liquorice Legs

Of course you can drink tea whenever you feel like it, but some of our blends are especially suited to different times of day – to pick you up, calm you down and help you drift off at night.

French Earl Grey

Green Rose

White Rose

Gone Surfing

What do you see?

a) A cat
b) Trees
c) Two fish kissing
d) A butterfly
e) A macaron

---

e) If you see a macaron, you are hungry. Have it with Strawberries & Cream.
d) If you see a butterfly, your outgoing personality hides a tender side that needs nurturing. You should drink Sencha Sprinkles.
c) If you see two fish kissing, you are a people person who loves to connect with others in all kinds of ways. You should drink Chilli Kiss.
b) If you see trees, your ideas are rooted in reality but your dreams aim for the sky. You should drink Red Green Dreamy.
a) If you see a cat, you are an individual who values independence and striking out on your own. You should drink New York Breakfast.

Chairs

Gone Surfing

White Rose

Choc Chip Chai

Strawberries & Cream

Melbourne Breakfast

Grand Yunnan

Liquorice Legs

Sencha Sensation

Glasses

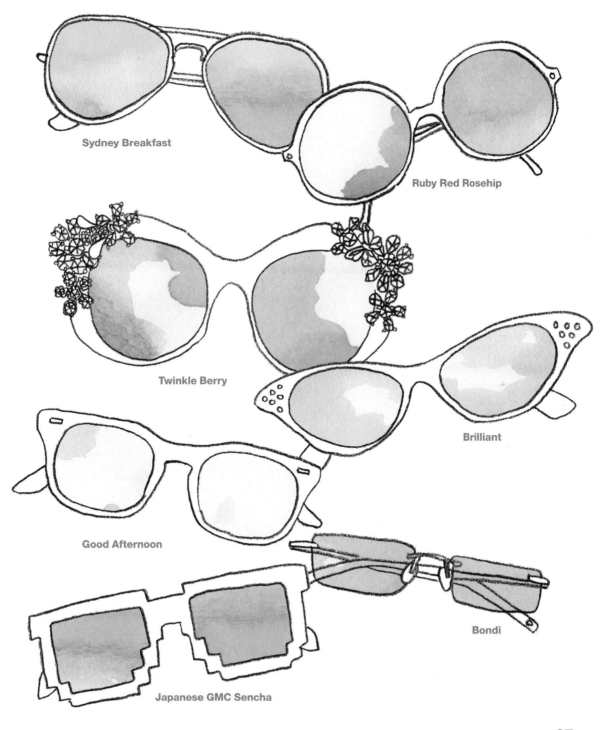

Sydney Breakfast

Ruby Red Rosehip

Twinkle Berry

Brilliant

Good Afternoon

Bondi

Japanese GMC Sencha

Hairstyles

Fruit Blush

Honey Honey

Lung Ching Classic

Really Russian Caravan

Ti Kuan Yin

Passion

Red Fancy Fruit

Ayurvedic Vata Boom

Which tea are you?

Good Morning

Breakfast

Terrific Toffee

Favourite meal of the day?

Afternoon snack

Creme Brulee

Dessert

Dark and milky

Light and floral

Sweet and fruity

Perfect holiday?

A fun time is . . .

Paris

Gardening

Hiking

Bubble bath

Tokyo

Hawaii

Spring

French Earl Grey

Southern Sunrise

Sencha Peach

Just Jasmine

Gone Surfing

Tea ceremonies

We believe that every time a cup of tea is made it is a small ceremony.
You pour boiled water over the leaves, then pause and let them brew.
It's a moment of reflection.

Every country does tea differently and has its own tea ceremony.
The Japanese believe that the *chanoyu*, or tea ceremony, is not just
about tea but is 'a religion of the art of life'.

Asked by a disciple about the elements of the tea ceremony,
the great Japanese tea master, Sen no Rikyū, said:

> Make a delicious bowl of tea
> Lay out the wood charcoal to heat the water
> Arrange the flowers as they are in the fields
> In summer, evoke coolness, in winter, warmth
> Anticipate the time for everything
> Be prepared for rain
> Show the greatest attention to each of your guests.

(PSST...)
LET THE TEA DO THE
TALKING

The Chinese way of tea, known as 'cha dao', has been influenced by the
philosophies of Tao, Buddha and Confucius.

In China today, tea is frequently brewed using the Gong Fu method.
This term refers to skill acquired through practice, expertise gained from
repetition rather than talent.

Everything in a Gong Fu tea service is small and delicate, emphasising
the elegance of the tea. Oolong tea is preferred here; the leaves are steeped
repeatedly to intensify the flavour as they gradually unfurl.

After the tea is drunk, it is very important to ward off bad Qi (life force)
by neatly folding your table napkin. And in southern China, it is common
to thank the person serving the tea by knocking on the table with your three
middle fingers.

In Korea, tea drinking is viewed as a spiritual activity leading to higher
levels of inner awakening. Monks drink tea to help them meditate and offer
tea to the Buddha three times every day.

As a girl growing up in Australia, I remember the kettle was always on
and it felt like we drank tea all day. Our ceremony was a very straightforward
one – a kettle on the stove and a box of Lan-choo tea on the table, along with
a milk jug and white sugar. Sometimes we would have three sugars. Looking
back, this was a sweet, milky drink and you could hardly taste the tea, but
it didn't matter. I would sit down with my mum and my nan, and we would
just stop and sip. They are beautiful memories. ■

Tea around the world

China

In China, the tea ceremony is all about the tea itself – how it tastes, smells and the consistency from one cup to the next. The first infusion is steeped for less than a minute before being poured into the cups in one continuous circular motion. This ensures all the cups taste the same. After steeping, the tea is poured into a second teapot to drink at leisure. The original pot can be refilled up to five times, adding a little extra time for steeping each brew. Oolong tea is most commonly used.

Hong Kong

Roadside teahouses in Hong Kong used to offer small dumplings with their tea, and the two have become inseparable. Locals like to start the day with tea and dim sum while they socialise and read the paper. The meal is known as yum cha, which translates as 'drink tea'! Milk tea, made using a blend of black teas, evaporated milk and sugar, is a very popular way to serve tea in Hong Kong.

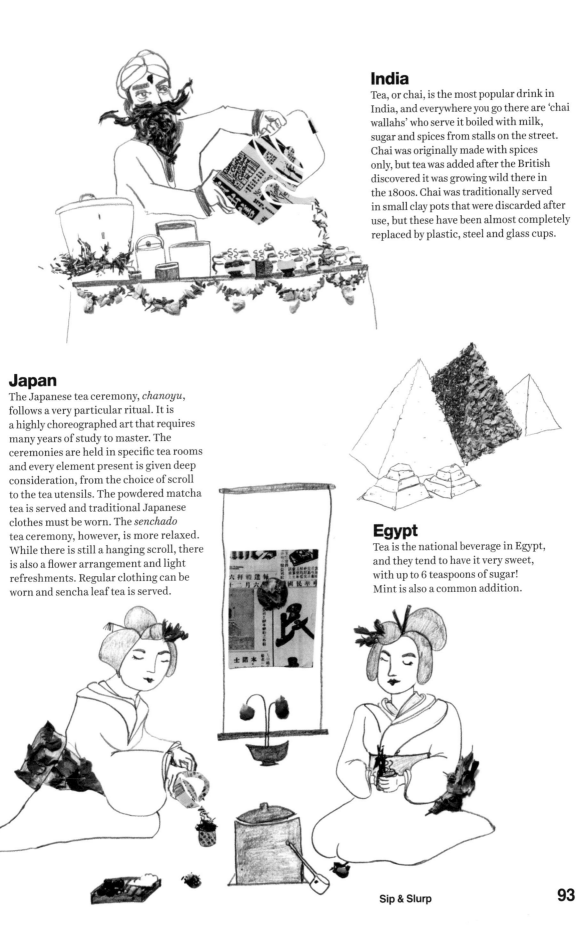

India

Tea, or chai, is the most popular drink in India, and everywhere you go there are 'chai wallahs' who serve it boiled with milk, sugar and spices from stalls on the street. Chai was originally made with spices only, but tea was added after the British discovered it was growing wild there in the 1800s. Chai was traditionally served in small clay pots that were discarded after use, but these have been almost completely replaced by plastic, steel and glass cups.

Japan

The Japanese tea ceremony, *chanoyu*, follows a very particular ritual. It is a highly choreographed art that requires many years of study to master. The ceremonies are held in specific tea rooms and every element present is given deep consideration, from the choice of scroll to the tea utensils. The powdered matcha tea is served and traditional Japanese clothes must be worn. The *senchado* tea ceremony, however, is more relaxed. While there is still a hanging scroll, there is also a flower arrangement and light refreshments. Regular clothing can be worn and sencha leaf tea is served.

Egypt

Tea is the national beverage in Egypt, and they tend to have it very sweet, with up to 6 teaspoons of sugar! Mint is also a common addition.

Sip & Slurp   **93**

Britain

Tea is enormously popular in England, where it has been drunk for centuries. At first, it was restricted to coffee houses for men only, while the women gathered at home for tea parties. Anna, the seventh Duchess of Bedford, sparked the trend for 'afternoon tea' in the 1840s by having buttered bread and cakes with her tea to tide her over until dinner. A traditional afternoon tea starts with savoury finger sandwiches, followed by scones and then a selection of cakes, all washed down with tea served in the best china. Etiquette dictates that all fingers should be curled around the handle of the cup – no pinkies sticking out!

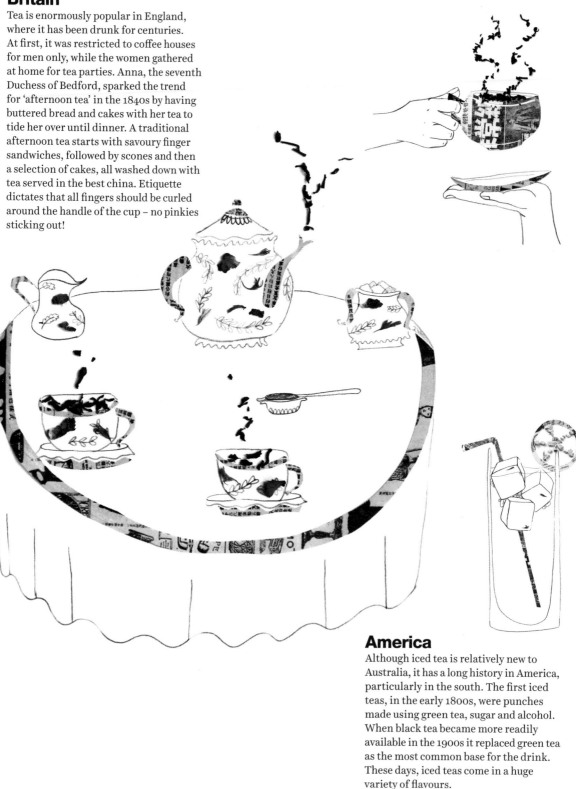

America

Although iced tea is relatively new to Australia, it has a long history in America, particularly in the south. The first iced teas, in the early 1800s, were punches made using green tea, sugar and alcohol. When black tea became more readily available in the 1900s it replaced green tea as the most common base for the drink. These days, iced teas come in a huge variety of flavours.

Morocco

When tea is being served in Morocco, first incense is lit to refresh the air and spirit, then hands are washed before the tea is poured. Mint tea, made from green tea and mint leaves sweetened with sugar, is taken several times a day. It is always poured from a height to make little bubbles that collect on the surface of the tea.

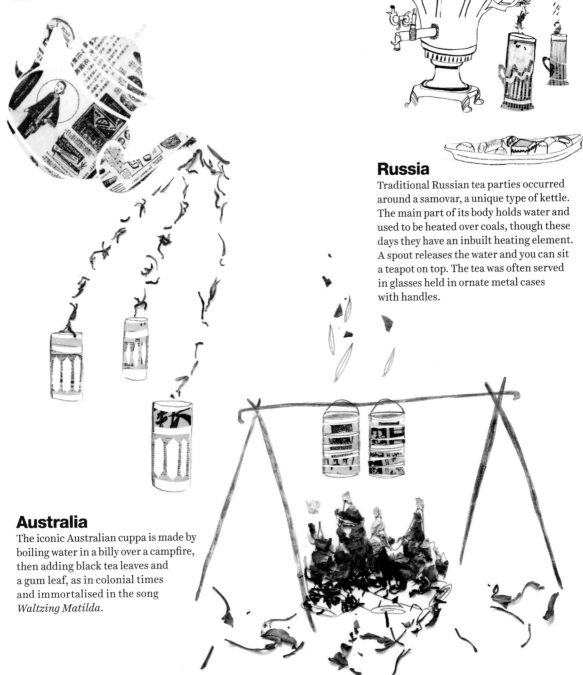

Russia

Traditional Russian tea parties occurred around a samovar, a unique type of kettle. The main part of its body holds water and used to be heated over coals, though these days they have an inbuilt heating element. A spout releases the water and you can sit a teapot on top. The tea was often served in glasses held in ornate metal cases with handles.

Australia

The iconic Australian cuppa is made by boiling water in a billy over a campfire, then adding black tea leaves and a gum leaf, as in colonial times and immortalised in the song *Waltzing Matilda*.

T2
NOW

2 o'clock
rush
hour cold brew
ck tea with apple,
nberry, hibiscus

Super tea

By Catherine Saxelby, accredited nutritionist and dietitian

The health benefits of drinking tea have long been appreciated. Tea is a natural source of powerful antioxidants known collectively as flavonoids, which belong to the general class of polyphenols (a large group of bio-active compounds in vegetables including onions, fruits, tea, cocoa and wine). The amount and type of flavonoids in tea depends on the variety, the amount of tea used and how long you brew your tea.

White, green, black and oolong teas all come from the same bush, *Camellia sinensis*. The difference lies in the way they are processed (traditionally known as 'fermented' or oxidised) after picking. Green tea leaves, due to their minimal processing, retain most of the simple tea flavonoids, known as catechins. Black teas are left to undergo oxidation, which changes the colour of the leaves to a rich golden-brown and converts the simple catechins to longer, more complex types called theaflavins and thearubigins. Oolong lies in between the two.

Tea is good for the heart

Drinking tea regularly can keep your heart in good working order. Research shows that drinking three cups of tea per day decreases the risk of heart attack by 11 per cent. This is due to those tea flavonoids, which maintain heart health by decreasing inflammation, lowering the tendency for clotting (an early factor in heart attacks) and keeping the arteries more 'elastic' so your blood flows freely. Adding milk or lemon to the brew makes no difference.

Tea can relax and revive

Tea has long been valued for its ability to both relax and refresh without the adrenalin 'jolt' that you can get from coffee. Scientists now believe it's due to theanine, a natural amino acid that works in conjunction with the caffeine in tea, and allows you to concentrate despite distractions.

A healthy thirst quencher

After water, tea is the most widely consumed beverage in the world,
so it's not surprising that tea is a refreshing way to relieve a thirst.
Tea is a hydrating liquid and counts towards our recommended intake
of 2 litres of fluid a day. Taken without milk or sugar, tea contains virtually
no kilojoules/calories.

Tea and caffeine

Tea does contains caffeine, but at a much lower concentration than coffee.
For example, a standard cup of black tea has less than half the amount of
caffeine (about 10–50 mg) than that in a cup of instant coffee (60–100 mg).

When the caffeine levels of tea and coffee are matched, research shows
that alertness is actually more consistent in individuals consuming tea,
thanks to the theanine in tea, which works synergistically with caffeine.

While it is true that too much caffeine can dehydrate the body, you
would have to drink five or six cups of tea at a single sitting for this to occur.
Nutritionists also now understand that people who drink caffeinated
drinks regularly often develop a tolerance to it, so the initial diuretic effect
is diminished. ■

Brain
Think sharper
Tea can improve cognitive function (thinking ability) thanks to its caffeine and theanine content, as well as through hydration.

Less chance of stroke
Drinking tea (2–4 cups per day) is associated with a 10–20 per cent lower risk of stroke.

Heart
Maintain heart health
The flavonoids in black tea have been shown to have a beneficial effect on the function of the endothelium (the inner lining of arteries), and so contribute to reduced arterial stiffness, indicating a better cardiovascular health profile.

Kidneys
Keep the kidneys working
All types of teas flush water through the system, especially in hot humid weather or when you've been sweating a lot.

Skin
Protect your skin
Green tea protects against UV light-induced DNA damage. It reduces skin inflammation, cell proliferation and tumour promoters. It slows sun damage and ageing.

Abdomen/stomach
Prevent abdominal fat
Green tea helps with weight loss from the middle (visceral fat) by speeding up fat oxidation. May improve the symptoms of metabolic syndrome in obese patients. Herbal teas aid digestion and settle queasy stomachs.

Blood vessels
Flex those vessels
Scientists believe that the flavonoids in tea work by relaxing blood vessels, which allows the blood to flow more evenly and become more 'elastic'.

Tea tastes better than a tablet

Headache

Indigestion

Insomnia

Nausea

Head cold

Hangover

Fatigue

Sunburn

Gone Surfing, Nighty Night
Try chamomile tea – it helps relax the mind and ease headaches. Or try chamomile blended with valerian root, lavender or skullcap (related to mint), which are all relaxants and help reduce feelings of anxiety.

Mint Mix, Soothe, Tummy Tea
Peppermint or spearmint teas can aid digestion and settle an upset stomach or one that's seen too much food and alcohol.

Sleep Tight
Chamomile is well known for its mild sedative effect and soothing properties. Lemon verbena also helps induce sleep. Herbal tisanes and rooibos are caffeine-free, so they're your best choice in the evening.

Just Ginger, Lemongrass and Ginger
Ginger helps overcome nausea and has long been recommended for morning sickness during pregnancy and motion sickness.

Just Chamomile
Place a handful of chamomile blossoms in a large bowl, add boiling water and leave to steep for 5 minutes before inhaling the steam. Like soup, hot tea is thought to help by liquefying and thinning mucus, making it easier to cough up or blow out.

Detox
Elderflower tea is often taken as a hangover cure. Any weak tea gives you water in an attractive-to-sip way, which is important to prevent dehydration, a major side effect of consuming excess alcohol.

Grand Yunnan, Darjeeling, Green Rose
Regular black and green tea, with their combination of natural theanine, polyphenol antioxidants and caffeine, revitalise and energise you after a busy day – one of the reasons for their enduring popularity.

English Breakfast
Applying a cloth soaked in strong, cold, black tea helps relieve the pain of sunburn and minimises skin damage.

Tea makes you feel good

Cooking with tea

At T2 HQ, we are united by our passion for tea and all that we can do with it. We occasionally have what we call 'pot luck', where everyone brings in their favourite savoury or sweet dish, and we put everything on the boardroom table and share it for lunch. It is a great opportunity to chat and have some time out. We recently added a twist – everything has to have tea in it!

If you haven't cooked with tea before, you might be surprised to learn that the subtle flavours of tea work beautifully in many different cuisines. Tea harmonises well with the sweetest of sweet or the most serious savoury, but it is also a delicious addition to jams, biscuits, ice-cream and more.

Sprinkling a little tea onto fish or meat before cooking adds texture and flavour – green tea goes particularly well with salmon. Or try smoking duck using lapsang souchong tea for a rich, aromatic flavour. You can soak dried fruit in tea or tisanes to use in a fruit cake for a nice flavour twist, or cool down on a hot day with icy poles made from your favourite fruit teas.

One of the most beautiful foods made with tea are Chinese tea eggs, hard-boiled eggs that are cracked, then soaked in black tea, spices and soy. During a recent visit to a tea estate in India's Darjeeling district, some of the T2 team tasted tea-leaf fritters (the recipe was from Christine Manfield's book, *Tasting India)* that used freshly picked leaves from this amazing region. They all raved about them on their return.

Matcha is a favourite tea of mine, more for its colour than its flavour. Taste-wise, it's powerful and bitter, and it is high in caffeine, but its bright-green colour is second to none and works brilliantly in ice-cream. You can also add fresh mint to matcha (or any green tea) ice-cream for a refreshing flavour combination. Matcha is used a lot in food – you might come across green-tea cake or bright-green macarons, even green-tea Kit Kats!

Here is a small selection of some of my favourite tea and food marriages. I hope they inspire you to grab some tea and start cooking.

Choc chip chai date loaf

By Kate Iles

Serve hot from the oven (we love it smothered with butter!), for an afternoon treat like no other. Add ½ cup (95 g) choc chips to the batter if you're feeling naughty. You can use regular Chai mix if you prefer, and you can change the orange zest to lemon zest.

Serves 8

4 scoops Choc Chip Chai mix
1 cup (250 ml) boiling water
2 cups (280 g) pitted dried dates, chopped
1 teaspoon bicarbonate of soda
¾ cup (165 g) brown sugar
150 g unsalted butter, melted and cooled
4 eggs
1½ teaspoons vanilla extract
1 teaspoon finely grated orange zest
½ teaspoon ground cinnamon
1¼ cups (185 g) self-raising flour
sifted icing sugar, for garnish

■ Preheat the oven to 170°C. Lightly grease a 23 x 12 cm loaf tin and line with baking paper.

■ Add the chai mix to the boiling water and set aside for 3 minutes. Strain the liquid, discarding the chai mix. Combine the brewed chai, dates and bicarbonate of soda in a small heatproof bowl and set aside for 10 minutes. Transfer to a small food processor or use a stick mixer to blend until smooth.

■ Put the brown sugar, butter, eggs, vanilla, orange zest and cinnamon into a bowl and use an electric mixer to beat until smooth and combined.

■ Sift the flour over the butter mixture and mix until combined. Mix in the date mixture. Spoon into the prepared tin and bake for 40–50 minutes or until a skewer inserted into the centre of the loaf comes out clean. Leave in the tin for 10 minutes to cool slightly before turning out onto a wire rack.

■ Serve warm or at room temperature, dusted with icing sugar.

Rooibos pumpkin bites

By Kate Iles

The trick to serving these bites is getting them to the table without eating them on the way.

Serves 4–6 as a side dish

olive oil, for drizzling
60 g unsalted butter
1 tablespoon Rooibos tea leaves
2 medium–large butternut pumpkins (squash)
1½ teaspoons Rooibos tea leaves, extra
1 teaspoon fine sea salt
freshly ground black pepper

■ Preheat the oven to 220°C and lightly oil 2 large baking trays with olive oil.

■ Heat a small frying pan over medium heat and add the butter and tea leaves. When the butter foams, remove the pan from the heat, cover and set aside for 10 minutes to infuse. Strain the butter through a fine sieve, discarding the tea leaves.

■ Meanwhile, using a large, sharp knife, cut off the stems and seedless 'necks' of the pumpkins (save the seeded parts for another use). Stand each neck cut-side down and slice off the skin using seven or eight cuts, leaving a kind of octagonal shape. Cut the necks into 1 cm thick slices and place on the greased trays, spaced slightly apart.

■ Pulverise the extra tea leaves (if they are already fine, skip this step) and mix with the salt. Brush the infused butter over the pumpkin, then season with pepper and half the rooibos salt. Bake for about 25 minutes or until very soft. Transfer to a platter and sprinkle with the remaining rooibos salt.

Lapsang souchong tea eggs

By Michelle McGoff

An afternoon snack, a breakfast treat, or served in ramen, these tea eggs look good and taste even better.

Makes 8

3 cups (750 ml) water
150 ml soy sauce
½ cup (110 g) caster sugar
3 star anise
2 cinnamon sticks
4 thick strips of mandarin peel
1 tablespoon Lapsang Souchong tea leaves
8 eggs

■ Combine the water, soy sauce, sugar, star anise, cinnamon sticks and mandarin peel in a large saucepan and bring to the boil. Remove from the heat, add the tea leaves and set aside for 20 minutes to steep.

■ Meanwhile, fill a large saucepan with cold water, add the eggs and bring to the boil. Cook the eggs for 4 minutes, then use a slotted spoon to transfer to a bowl of cold water. Leave the eggs until they are cool enough to handle.

■ Crack the egg shells using the back of a spoon, but don't remove the shells. This will create the marbling effect – the deeper the cracks, the darker the effect will be. Place the eggs in the tea mixture and bring to the boil. Cook, stirring occasionally, for 10 minutes, then remove from the heat. Cover the pan and leave the eggs to cool in the marinade overnight. Store the unpeeled eggs in an airtight container in the fridge for up to 5 days.

Tea-smoked trout

By Nicola Shimmin

Delicately flaked and served on rye crackers, this tea-smoked trout reminds us of chilly nights on the coast with a fire crackling and warm tea in our hands.

Serves 6

2 teaspoons Red Earl Grey tea leaves
2 cups (500 ml) boiling water
1 tablespoon fresh honeycomb (or brown sugar)
1 teaspoon smoked paprika
1 tablespoon rock salt
1 whole wild brown trout, cleaned
½ cup Lapsang Souchong tea leaves
mesquite and alder wood chips, for smoking
rye crackers, to serve

■ Add the tea leaves to the boiling water and honeycomb (or sugar) and leave to brew for 10 minutes. Strain, discarding the tea leaves and allow to cool. Add the paprika and salt and place in a non-reactive container with the trout (make sure it is well covered). Cover and marinate in the fridge overnight.

■ The next day, rinse the trout and place in a hot smoker with the lapsang souchong tea leaves, mesquite and alder wood chips. Smoke for 40–45 minutes. Serve hot or cool in the fridge. Delicious flaked on rye crackers – use any leftovers to make a smoked trout dip.

Green tea ice cream

By Magenta Burgin

Like a matcha latte in frozen form ... a double scoop might not be enough!

Serves 4

1½ cups (375 ml) full-cream milk
1 cup (250 ml) thickened cream
5 egg yolks
2 tablespoons Matcha green tea powder
½ cup (110 g) caster sugar
½ teaspoon Gyokuro tea leaves, for garnish

■ Place the milk and cream in a saucepan and heat over medium heat until almost boiling, then remove from the heat and set aside.

■ Use an electric mixer to beat the egg yolks and sugar until the sugar is dissolved and the mixture is pale yellow. Sift in the matcha and mix well.

■ Return the milk and cream mixture to low–medium heat and slowly add the egg mixture, stirring constantly with a wooden spoon until the mixture has thickened to a custard consistency and coats the back of the spoon.

■ Transfer the mixture to a bowl, then place in a larger bowl of iced water until cooled. Remove the bowl from the iced water, cover with plastic film and chill in the fridge for 2–3 hours.

■ Transfer the mixture to an ice-cream maker and churn following the manufacturer's instructions.

■ Serve the ice cream sprinkled lightly with the gyokuro leaves.

Chai shortbread

By Alexandra Oke

Cute as pie, but tasty as chai.

Makes about 15

150 g butter, softened at room temperature
⅔ cup (150 g) caster sugar
½ teaspoon vanilla extract
2 cups (300 g) plain flour
pinch of salt
1 tablespoon Chai mix, finely ground
1½ cups (285 g) chocolate chips

■ In a large mixing bowl, cream the butter and sugar until light and fluffy. Add the vanilla and blend well.

■ In a separate bowl, combine the flour, salt and chai mix and fluff with a fork or whisk.

■ Add the dry ingredients to the butter mixture and mix until the ingredients come together – the dough should be a bit crumbly. Mould the dough into a 20 cm log, wrap in plastic film and place in the fridge for at least 1 hour, or in the freezer for 20 minutes, until firm.

■ Preheat the oven to 180°C and line a baking tray with baking paper.

■ Using a serrated knife, cut the dough into 1.5 cm thick discs and place 5 cm apart on the prepared tray. Bake for 12 minutes or until lightly golden, then remove and set aside to cool. If you like, as we did in the photo, you can cut the cookies into tea-bag shapes before they cool.

■ While the cookies are cooling, place the chocolate chips in a heatproof bowl set over a saucepan of barely simmering water. Stir until the chocolate has melted, then remove from the heat.

■ Dip the cookies into the melted chocolate to coat one half. Return to the tray to set.

New York breakfast sticky date pudding

By Steven Nash

Dessert for breakfast in New York or New York Breakfast in a dessert? We'll take both, please!

Serves 8

1 tablespoon New York Breakfast tea leaves
1 cup (250 ml) boiling water
1½ cups (210 g) chopped pitted dates
1 teaspoon bicarbonate of soda
100 g butter, chopped
¾ cup (165 g) brown sugar
2 eggs
1 cup (150 g) self-raising flour
thick cream, to serve

Toffee sauce
150 g butter, chopped
1 cup (250 ml) pouring cream
1½ cups (330 g) brown sugar

■ Preheat oven to 180°C and lightly grease 8 holes of a regular muffin tin.

■ Brew the tea in the boiling water for 3 minutes, then discard the leaves. Combine the tea with the dates and bicarbonate of soda in a bowl and allow to stand for 5 minutes. Transfer to the bowl of a food processor, add the butter and sugar and mix until well combined.

■ Add the eggs and flour and process until just combined. Pour the batter into the greased muffin holes and bake for 30–35 minutes or until a skewer inserted in the centre comes out clean. Cool in the tin for 10 minutes, then transfer to individual serving plates.

■ Meanwhile, to make the toffee sauce, place the butter, cream and sugar in a saucepan over medium heat and stir until the butter has melted. Bring to the boil and cook for 5 minutes or until thickened slightly. Spoon over the puddings and serve with thick cream.

Tea-infused mousse

By Melanie Puckey

Earl Grey and dark chocolate are made for each other in the same way that chai and white chocolate are meant to be. The only thing that makes these pairings even better is eating them in mousse form!

Serves 10

1 heaped teaspoon tea leaves (such as Earl Grey for the dark chocolate mousse or Chai for white chocolate)
100 ml boiling water
½ cup (110 g) caster sugar
2 teaspoons finely grated orange zest
250 g good-quality chocolate (dark, milk or white), broken into pieces
6 eggs, separated
pinch of salt
whipped cream or mascarpone, to serve
coarsely grated orange zest or cinnamon stick shards, to garnish (optional)

■ Infuse the tea in the boiling water for 4 minutes. Stir in the sugar and orange zest until the sugar has dissolved.

■ Place the chocolate in a heatproof bowl set over a saucepan of barely simmering water. Stir until the chocolate has melted, then remove from the heat and allow to cool slightly.

■ Whisk the egg whites and salt in a blender, mixer or food processer for 5–10 minutes until stiff peaks form. Transfer to a large bowl.

■ Stir the tea mixture into the chocolate, then add the egg yolks and blend or mix for 10 seconds. Gently fold this mixture into the egg whites using a spatula.

■ Pour the mousse into 10 individual bowls or one large bowl and refrigerate for 3–4 hours until set. The mousse can be made up to a day in advance, if liked. Serve with whipped cream or mascarpone, garnished with orange zest (for the earl grey mousse) or cinnamon (for the chai mousse), if using.

Brick lane chai

By John Thompson

This big mug of deliciousness reminds us of the old streets of London. It's a mecca of sweet and spice.

Makes 1 litre

1 tablespoon Chai mix
1 tablespoon Toasty Nougat mix
2 teaspoons Cocoa Loco mix
1 teaspoon Secret Spices mix
1 teaspoon honey
2 cups (500 ml) boiling water
2 cups (500 ml) vanilla soy milk, hot
chocolate powder, to garnish

■ Place all the teas and honey in the infuser basket of a 1 litre teapot. Pour over the boiling water and allow to brew for 5 minutes. Remove the infuser and discard the leaves.

■ Add the soy milk to the teapot and mix well. Serve garnished with chocolate powder.

Pomegranate sunrise

By John Thompson

A brew that whisks us away on a tropical vacation and makes us want to hula dance.

Makes 2 litres

700 ml boiling water
1 tablespoon honey
juice of 1 lime
2 tablespoons Pumping Pomegranate mix
2 tablespoons Southern Sunrise mix
ice cubes
lime slices, to garnish

■ Pour the boiling water into a 2 litre iced tea jug. Add the honey and lime juice and stir until the honey has dissolved.

■ Place the tea mixes in the infuser and attach to the lid, then submerge in the hot water and brew for 5 minutes. Remove the infuser and discard the tea leaves. Fill the jug with ice and serve garnished with lime slices.

T2 life

People often say that T2 has a unique culture. Part of it is our desire to do things differently – to shake up the world of tea and make it young, modern and exciting. But a large part of it is the fact that we are not motivated by money. Everything we do is about the experience, the team, the tea and the customer. We want our team to be inspired to grow the T2 tea generation, not to make sales. T2 is all about passion, that is our driver.

When we started T2, we wanted to reinvent the category of tea. In the same way, we now look for collaborators who have broken the mould in their own industry. It's a totally spontaneous process – we will be talking about design or leafing through a magazine and suddenly we'll come across someone who is exciting and inspiring. We invite passionate people to tell us what they love about tea and we turn that into an experience.

One such collaboration was with renowned Australian fashion designer Akira Isogawa, who was born in Japan and whose designs reflect that aesthetic. When we invited Akira to create a tea set, he was about to set off for Kyoto to visit his family home. On his return he gave us a beautiful Japanese pot, some classic Japanese tea and a favourite kimono. This was all we needed to create a little bit of Akira in our T2 world.

We recently worked with talented ceramicist Samantha Robinson, whose creations are beautifully crafted and feature exquisite decorative patterns. Samantha works from the heart and her products are all about the hand. We discovered her ceramics, gave her a call and she came to our office where we clicked instantly.

Samantha started producing new shapes and patterns to complement the T2 brand. She presented a sample range, then the final selection was made and production began using a co-branded logo. All Samantha's designs are handmade and hand-painted, and T2 customers around the globe have embraced the collection.

Another successful collaboration has been with the highly regarded ceramic studio Iggy & Lou Lou. They're known for creating limited-edition, numbered and handmade products, and the unique nature of their creations complements T2's contemporary teawares. ❑

Courtney Gibbs/ Architect

Courtney reminds us of a perfectly brewed cup of Gyokuro – refined and complex, with a vibrant finish that livens our day and inspires greatness.

Your idea of happiness?
Warm sunlight and fresh air with friends somewhere in Italy.

Favourite destination?
Japan, specifically Nishizawa Teshima Art Museum.

Greatest source of inspiration?
Modernism, raw materials, nature, Lina Bo Bardi, Google image searches and great people.

Courtney drinks . . .
Melbourne Breakfast in the morning, Liquorice Legs at night and Ruby Red Rosehip on weekends.

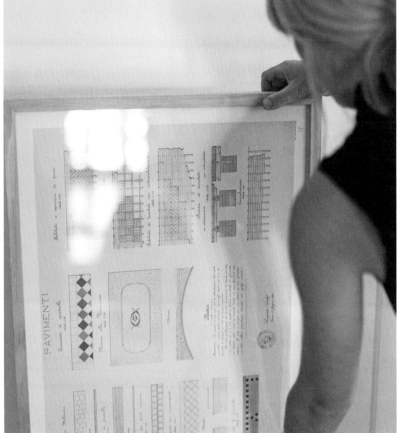

Theo Hassett/ Shoemaker

In the way that tea and leather have tannins in common, T2 and Theo share a love for a big cup of Melbourne Breakfast (and beautiful shoes).

Favourite destination?
A body of water on a hot day.

Most treasured possession?
It's all just stuff.

Weekend ritual?
I try to keep it varied.

Theo drinks . . .
Japanese Sencha.

Chris Odrowaz/ Barista

Chris makes a killer chai! It's so good that he won our 2014 Chai Championship and a tea trip to India.

Most memorable holiday?
I went to Vietnam in 2013, bought a motorbike and travelled all the way from the south to the Chinese border.

Your idea of happiness?
Simply friends, family and food.

Morning ritual?
Starting the day with a solid breakfast.

Chris drinks . . .
Oolong and Chai.

Olivia Nelson/ T2 Teawares Buyer

Olivia knows a good cup and saucer. She travels the world and brings back weird and wonderful treasures that make tea taste even better.

Favourite destination?
Berlin.

Greatest source of inspiration?
Textiles and art with a little bit of life.

Most treasured possession?
Memories, I don't really have a material one.

Olivia drinks . . .
Ruby Red Rosehip and Lemongrass and Ginger.

Samantha Robinson/ Ceramicist

Samantha's teawares elevate a daily brew to a moment worth savouring. It's a little reminder for us to find beauty in the everyday.

Daily treat?
Chocolate, good music.

Your idea of happiness?
Summer, sunshine, swimming in the ocean with my kids, butterflies and roses.

Greatest source of inspiration?
Flowers, fabrics, nature and the everyday.

Samantha drinks . . .
Ruby Red Rosehip, White Rose and Gyokuro.

Kristina Karlsson/ kikki.K Founder

Kristina is every bit the Scandi dream, as is the Swedish Söder Tea we made with her. Her home is a minimalist retreat of clean lines and enviable organisation.

Favourite destination?
Our home in Falkenberg, Sweden – it's such a 'family happy place' for us.

Words to live by?
Enjoy the little things, as one day they'll likely be the big things.

Greatest source of inspiration?
Travel, reading, food, restaurants, bars, art, shopping, photography.

Kristina drinks . . .
T2 Earl Grey – at home every morning and when I travel I always take some with me.

145

Iggy & Lou Lou/ Ceramicists

Talking teaware with Irene and Peter Selzer from Iggy & Lou Lou makes our heart flutter. We got lost somewhere between romantic, whimsical, rare and made to keep forever.

Greatest source of inspiration?
Life – couldn't really pin down one aspect.

Your idea of happiness?
Doing things or nothings all together.

Morning ritual?
We have two small children, so looking after them is our morning ritual!

Irene and Peter drink . . .
Chocolate mint tea – we grow the herb on our windowsill and make tea out of it.

Evi O./
Book
Designer

Evi has been our
tour guide and travel
buddy in the journey
to create this book.
Doing it without her
would be like facing
a day without a cup of
White Rose (and that's
a scary thought).

Favourite destination?
New York.

Favourite book?
**Anything by
Haruki Murakami.**

Dream Project?
**One that involves
people I admire.**

Evi drinks . . .
**White Rose, Pai Mu Tan
and Gyokuro.**

150

Tin & Ed/ Creative Directors & Artists

Experimentation is something T2 holds dear and it's with a similar spirit of curiosity and play that Tin & Ed produce work that makes us want to wear colour (that's big!).

Dream project?
Something with NASA or David Attenborough, also any project which involves something we can eat or drink.

Stress relief?
Being in nature.

Best day ever?
That day we found oysters and ate them straight off the rocks.

Tin & Ed drink . . .
Buddha's Tears and Silver Needles.

T2
Story

T2 is a place where all
tea lovers come together.
— Jaime Ireland

T2 is a sensory playground
with genuinely passionate people,
a hub of innovation and experiment,
pushing the boundaries of tea creativity. — Heath Barrett

What is

T2 is merging the
'old world charm' of tea
to the modern lifestyle.

T2 is a girl.
— jessica tate
She is dynamic,
bold, energetic, passionate,
eclectic. She is also subtle,
reflective and sensitive... most of all
she is fun!
— Kate Iles.

family!
– Kristen Shearer

To me, T2 is home. Having the pleasure to grow + develop while T2 does the same has been an incredibly unique experience. Names and faces may have changed over time but there has always been one constant; brew up a pot and anyone will be happy to join you for a cup and a chat, a laugh or a tear.
–Scott Yurisich

T2?

T2 is life and art woven together. T2 is the homage of tea, of things new and old. T2 is family, a place to discuss + taste. –Meredith O'Neil.

A community of people open to new possibilities for an ancient tradition. An innovator. The gateway to the new world of tea in all its forms and opportunities
– Nick Beckett

T2 experience

T2 is a performer: our stores are the stage and everything on that stage is there to excite and enchant the customer.

Tea drinking, largely because of its long history and ancient traditions, has become a very serious pursuit. Our aim at T2 is to break the rules that have been established over thousands of years of tea drinking and reinvent the way the world thinks about tea.

We believe that tea is wild, delightful and delicious, and we want to celebrate that. We have only one rule and that is to find the tastiest brew at any given time of the day.

We design our stores to be welcoming, embracing and theatrical. When a customer is in our store we don't want them to leave – not because we want them to spend money, but because we have so much to share with them, from tastings to tea stories and tea knowledge. Once a customer is committed to entering our store it is up to our team to keep them interested for long enough to fall in love with tea all over again. The trick for us is inviting the customer into the store from the street or mall.

Each year, we plan a 12-month experience calendar, a schedule of our performances if you like. Every six weeks T2 transforms itself with a new experience where everything changes, including the window display, tastings, feature teas, music, team uniforms, and so on. This transformation is critical. As we all know, most of the time tea is purchased in a static supermarket environment. Many things at T2 remain the same, for example you'll find English Breakfast tea in exactly the same place every time you walk into the store, but around 20 per cent of the teas change, and it is those changes that help to create the theatre and the interest.

Our team are our 'T2 tea generation', they bring their very own version of tea to the customer. Their age is irrelevant, but it is vital that they are young at heart. It's an attitude that is important: they must be passionate and love what they do. We seek to recruit people who are experimental and playful, and enjoy breaking the rules while still maintaining a sense of respect for what they and others do. ∎

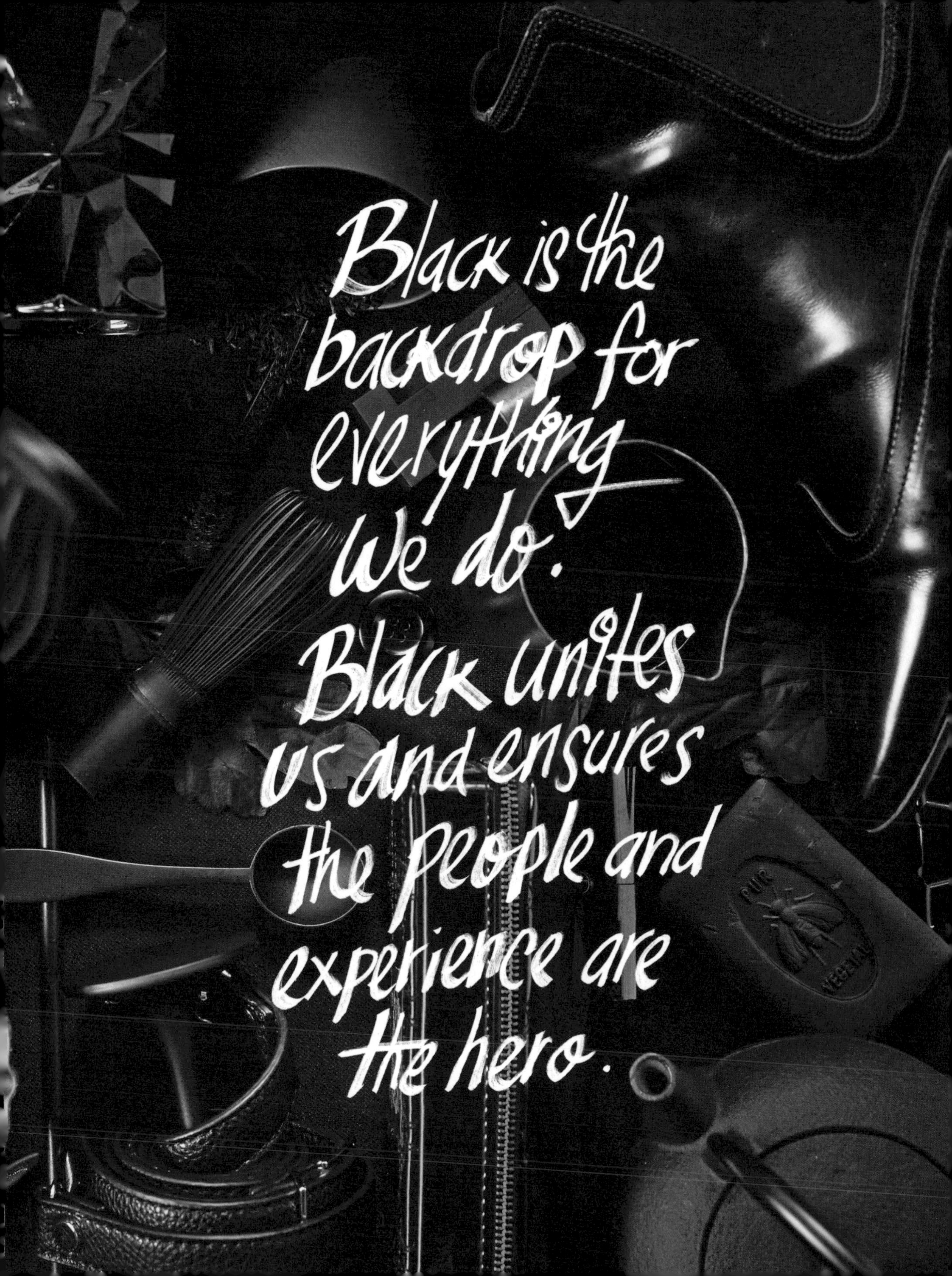

Black is the
backdrop for
everything
we do.
Black unites
us and ensures
the people and
experience are
the hero.

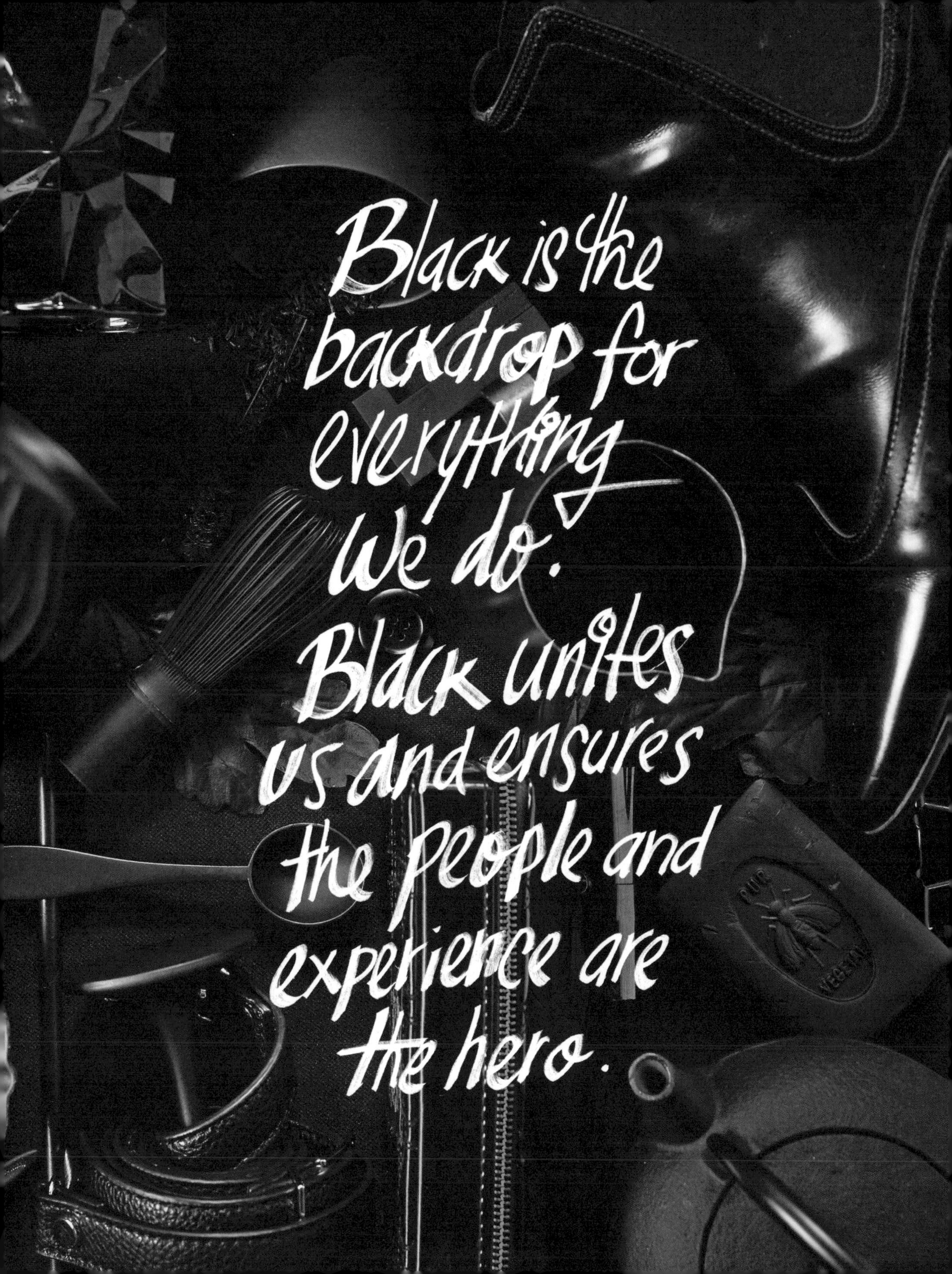

Black is the
backdrop for
everything
we do.
Black unites
us and ensures
the people and
experience are
the hero.

Our very early packaging had no creative thread – we were very experimental. It took us about 5 years to create any form of packaging discipline, but this was great as it gave us time to make mistakes and learn what worked for the brand.

Melbourne
Sydney
London
New York

Where to next?
Any place where the T2ers
like to visit, shop or
just hang out is
where we need to be.

T2 soundtrack (1996–2015)

Our defining moments are often marked by songs played too loud and on repeat for weeks.

2015 Romanticise – Chela
2014 Swingin Party – Kindness
2013 Wasting My Young Years – London Grammar
2012 Angels – The XX
2011 The Wilhelm Scream – James Blake
2010 Crave You – Flight Facilities
2009 Love Lost – The Temper Trap
2008 Skinny Love – Bon Iver
2007 Samson – Regina Spektor
2006 Hearts a Mess – Gotye
2005 Fix You – Coldplay
2004 Ten Days – Missy Higgins
2003 Relapse – Little Birdy
2002 You Give Me Something – Jamiroquai
2001 My Friend – Groove Armada
2000 Rome Wasn't Built in a Day – Morcheeba
1999 I Try – Macy Gray
1998 Teardrop – Massive Attack
1997 Over – Portishead
1996 Wrong – Everything But The Girl

T2 HQ

Behind every retailer there is always a large support crew, keeping the wheels turning in the background. T2 is no different and we chose Collingwood, Melbourne, as our home for the team to gather daily.

During the design process, we felt the space needed to be comfortable and relaxed. It was critical that when you walked in, there was tea being brewed and a friendly smile from our tea brewer who you could have a chat with and who could also point you in the right direction.

On the operational side of the building, we broke the space into left-brain (commercial support) and right-brain (customer touch). Creative and product teams are in a separate wing, as they work with longer timeframes and have very little to do with the operational side of the business.

We love our space, as it allows everyone to hide out and focus, or mingle and mix.

T2 Central is what most people would call 'reception'. This is where we greet you as you walk into our world. We make you a cup of tea, then help you connect with the person you are there to visit.

We do a lot of tea tasting, as opposed to tea drinking. We are always looking for great classic teas and enjoy subtle differences between estates. We love to create crazy blends using ingredients like banana, carrot and beetroot! We constantly bounce between serious and fun tea!

Our Tea Room is where we experiment and play. It's a place where anything is possible.

We have a display of big black tins containing our teas at T2 Central – they are the teas we love, the teas that will never date. Note we still don't call them our 'favourites'!

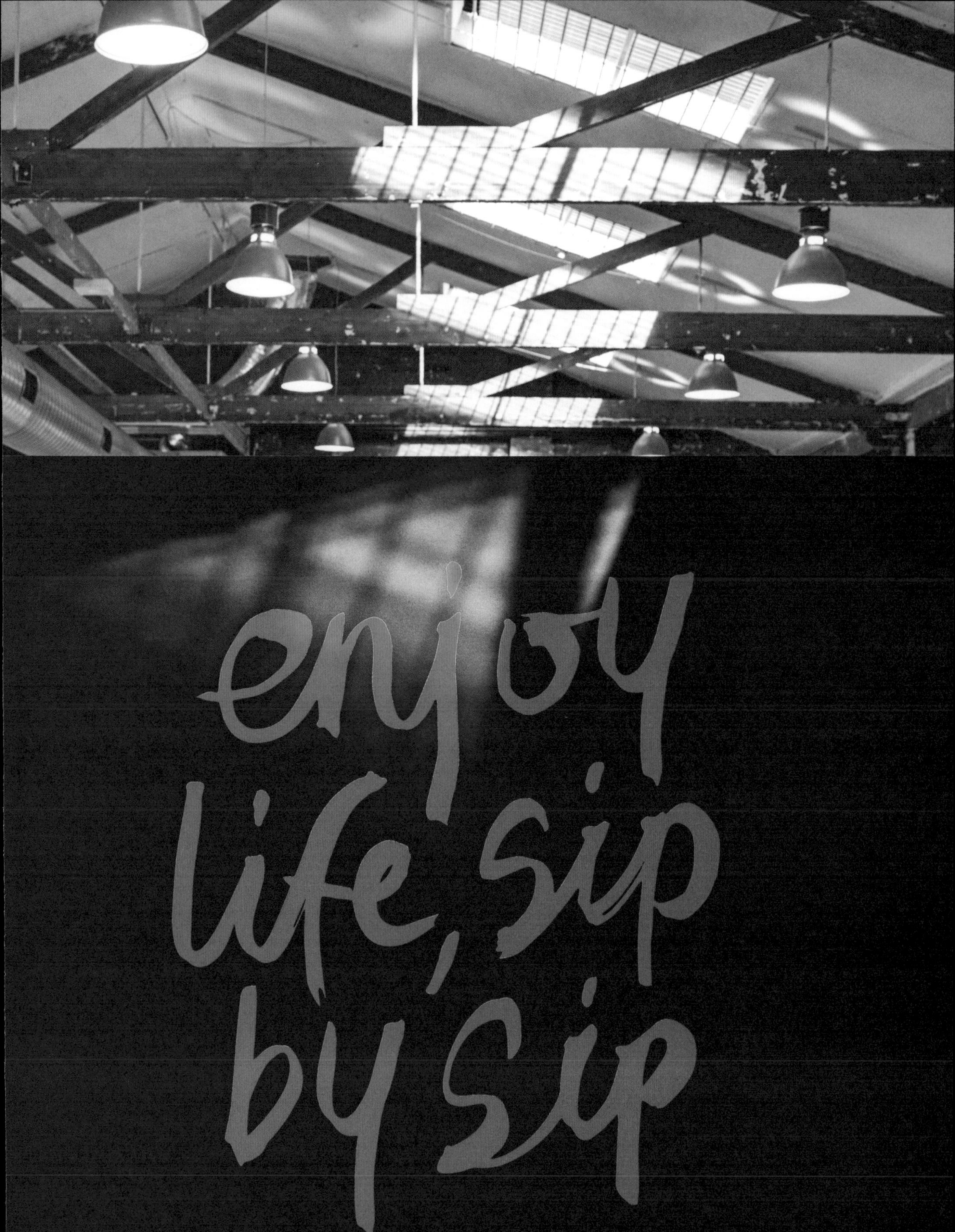
enjoy
life, sip
by sip

T2
Inspiration
(constant reinvention)

T2 doesn't look for inspiration, it actually just happens. Our mantra is 'constant reinvention'. We do not look to the world of tea for our inspiration, we look to the world in general. Art and music also play a very big part in what we do.

Scented + Floral

Scented tea is a base of black, green or whatever tea, then flowers or petals are added for a subtle flavour

Flavoured Tea

Flavoured tea is a base of black, green or whatever tea, then a nature identical flavour is added (sprayed) onto the tea.

While in Turkey we fell in love with these tea glasses that look like jewels. We just had to find a way to incorporate them into our display.

white jasmine

white monkey jasmine

toasty nougat

strawberries + cream

sikkim temi

rolling clouds

red earl grey

toasty warm

strawberry sensation

silver needles

ruby red rosehip

MYSELF.

T2 COOL
MELON HEAD

FUN
DIFFERENT
COMICAL
INTERESTING
COLOURFUL
QUIRKY

Cool Sorts - image

Imagery Bright colours, great production, and full of expression

T2
ICED TEA
RECIPES

I WA
LAU
I WA
CRY.

UST PLAYING
D-TEA TWISTER
H MY TEA-MATES
ANGO, APPLE
& THE BERRY!

T2 COOL
CASE

FANCY A BANAN
SMOOTHIE WITH
THOSE PANCAKES
ON ICE?

T2 COOL - B

I WANT TO
LAUGH,
I WANT TO
CRY.

SUPER CHILLED WITH
A JUICY GINGER KICKER?
WELL KNOCK ME OVER...

T2 COOL - JUICY GINGER

Photography - The beach

SUPER CHILLED WITH
A JUICY GINGER KICKER?
WELL KNOCK ME OVER...

I WANT TO
LAUGH,
I WANT TO
CRY.

Photography - The beach

This is one of the images from our 'Iced' campaign. Our moodboard for this is on the opposite page.

177

Marie Antoinette was the inspiration for our 'Marie Loves Tea' tea set. Lots of fun!

We get our inspiration from all sorts of things. When one of our team members pulled out her new wallet from Comme des Garçons, we fell in love and this tea set and packaging were born!

181

"The combined tastes of sour apples and tropical fruits are as crazy as Kid Creole and the Coconuts!"

"A hint of mango and a dash of rose dance together with perfect rhythm"

assionately layful and s pretty as punch"

DEATH CHAOS LIFE.

Bruce Weber Surfing's Fashion Pioneer

FROM BERLIN WITH LUV

T2 INTER- VIEW.

VOGUE PARIS

MODE ET ART

naughty and nice

Hang out and fall in love.

I think we're going to have to be secretly in love with each other and leave it at that.

What we imagine may be very beautiful, but nothing replaces reality.

READ MY

T2 Salsa

T2 Conga

READ MY

TRANSIENT ISCHAEMIC ATTACK PAINTING LONDON 1 (TIAPL1): THERE ARE NO FEMALE LEPRECHAUNS: WHICH WAY DOES A COMPASS POINT IN SPACE? FLY SPRAY

TOKYO 1969

This campaign was all about 'Passion'. A hot summer night, dancing on the beach, and pops of colour, as seen on our moodboard (see opposite page).

T2 generation

Nineteen years ago, when T2 was just an idea that we were trying to turn into a reality, we did our homework on what tea leaves to use, what packaging to create, and so on, but at no stage did we realise the future was actually about the people, the teams, the customers, the suppliers . . . In fact, anyone that even touched the brand slightly has become a critical team member in building this incredible new generation of tea drinkers. The 'T2 Generation' is a term we use for the thousands of people around the world who have become devoted to the way we do tea. We do it differently; we respect the traditions of tea absolutely, but always felt tea needed to be reinvented to seduce the younger generation.

T2's personality is bright and energetic. We are always ready for fun and love to share that fun with those around us. We are humble and respectful of others, and we don't like to talk about ourselves – we tend to be more of a storyteller, and after eighteen years doing what we do we have lots of stories to share. On that note, we do not advertise T2 products. We believe that if you spoil your customers, they will spread the word and we feel this is a genuine, organic way to share the T2 love around.

Our teams are not taught to sell, but are asked to inform and spoil their customer. When we go through our recruitment process we look for passion, not necessarily for tea, but for life. We're after positive, upbeat people with a hunger for newness, who like to be surprised and delighted and who like to surprise and delight others in turn. They just need to really love what they do.

As a result, our T2ers are passionate, energetic and ready for fun. They always go way above and beyond their defined jobs to look after our customers, so we felt it was important to give them something back in return. We didn't want it to be money; we wanted to thank them with an experience they would never forget. So, we created a program called T2 Heroes, in which six T2ers get to go on a tea-guided tour through some of the most beautiful, exotic tea origins in the world. Everyone comes back united and even more passionate about tea and, of course, T2. We always struggle a little to choose the six recipients, because we feel everyone at T2 is a hero, but it's become something the team really looks forward to every year. I love announcing the names, as it is simply a great big thanks because they are all awesome.

T2 has unfurled and blossomed over the years, and now sells enough tea per month to make 9 million cups! But behind all of that is our people, and we love them. To all of the T2 Generation, thank you. ■

This is a shot of me and my sister Kirsten. She is the person responsible for our obsession with putting the customer first, which led to unique initiatives like T2 Generation.

Welcome to
t2 Warringah's
Tea-Ki bar
leave your worries at
the door & join us!

T2 milestones

2007
T2 opened seven stores this year after consolidating for a few years, thereby creating a more robust business model.

2002
Knowing we were now trading strongly, we decided it was time to put in place a management team and structure that allowed us to realise our dream and become a national retailer.

1997
T2 wholesale kicked off by working closely with some of Melbourne's best restaurants.

2001
T2 opened its first store in Sydney in King St, Newtown.

July 1st 1996
T2 opened its first store at 340 Brunswick St, Fitzroy.

1999
T2 opened its third store in Chadstone Shopping Centre, a brave move but it was a great success and proved our brand has mass appeal.

1998
T2 opened its second store in Fitzroy St, St Kilda; this store would close only 12 months later due to poor trade.

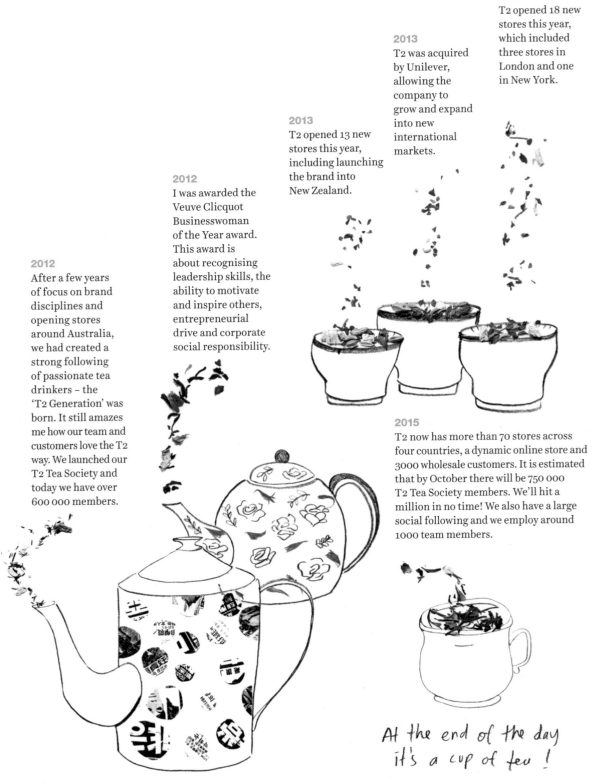

2014
T2 opened 18 new stores this year, which included three stores in London and one in New York.

2013
T2 was acquired by Unilever, allowing the company to grow and expand into new international markets.

2013
T2 opened 13 new stores this year, including launching the brand into New Zealand.

2012
I was awarded the Veuve Clicquot Businesswoman of the Year award. This award is about recognising leadership skills, the ability to motivate and inspire others, entrepreneurial drive and corporate social responsibility.

2012
After a few years of focus on brand disciplines and opening stores around Australia, we had created a strong following of passionate tea drinkers – the 'T2 Generation' was born. It still amazes me how our team and customers love the T2 way. We launched our T2 Tea Society and today we have over 600 000 members.

2015
T2 now has more than 70 stores across four countries, a dynamic online store and 3000 wholesale customers. It is estimated that by October there will be 750 000 T2 Tea Society members. We'll hit a million in no time! We also have a large social following and we employ around 1000 team members.

At the end of the day it's a cup of tea !

189

Acknowledgements

T2 The Book is simply a summary of 19 wonderful years of passionate people coming together to share tea stories and create our unique tea world.

The T2 team are the essence of the T2 brand and culture, and I thank you all from the bottom of my heart for making us bookworthy. In particular, I thank Kirsten Shearer, Nick Beckett and Bruce Crome for riding the highs but also the lows, for never doubting for one second that we would get there, and for putting up with my daily 'hey, I have a great idea' moments. If it weren't for these three people, there would be nothing to write a book about. I also thank Jan O'Connor, my original partner in T2.

I thank all of our suppliers for constantly pushing the boundaries and saying 'can do' when we asked for the impossible. Particular thanks go to Bill and Scott Bennett for the abundance of support and priceless tea knowledge you have shared over the years. Also Dietmar Scheffler and Tammo de Buhr: although you are all the way over in Hamburg it has always felt like you are standing right by our side, blending up the craziest combos or handing over precious little bundles of rare tea for us to enjoy and share.

Our 'T2 Life' partners who allowed us to come into their world and share their way of doing tea: thanks to Courtney Gibbs, Theo Hassett, Olivia Nelson, Chris, Samantha Robinson and team, Irene and Peter Selzer, Kristina Karlsson, Tin & Ed, and of course Evi O.

Thank you Julie Gibbs and the gang at Lantern Books, particularly Evi O., who really helped us close the book off in the end. Evi's playful approach to design and incredible knowledge of our brand made it so easy. The whole team at Lantern has been a treat to work with and their creative spirit and love of all things 'book' has been inspiring. Thanks also to Margot Saville the wordsmith, who unjumbled my words.

The in-house T2 'book team', especially Magenta Burgin (photography and styling) and Aleesha Maddern (coordination of just about everything), put in an intense home run, gathering bits and pieces from everywhere to make it all happen. We could not have pulled it together without you.

And finally, Nicky Sparshott and Amy Quinell and the rest of the team at Unilever have been so supportive of taking our tea ways to the world. Thank you all. ☐

Bruce and Maryanne in original Fitzroy office

191

Index

African tea, 31
Anna, Duchess of Bedford, 94
aroma, defined, 34
Assam tea plantations, 29
assamica varietal, 17, 32

Beckett, Nicholas, as CFO, 8–9
Bennett, Bill, 5
black as signature colour, 2
black tea
    brewing, 60–61
    directory, 71
    nutritional benefits, 101
    production of, 46
blooming tea, 50
Boston Tea Party, 20–21
breakfast teas, sugar with, 66
brewing tea, 58–63
broken-leaf teas, 18
builder's tea, 65

caffeine in tea, 102
cambodgiensis varietal, 17
Camellia sinensis, 17, 25, 32
Chadstone store, 6–7
Chai tea
    brewing, 61
    Brick Lane Chai, 127
    Choc Chip Chai Date Loaf, 111
    cooking with, 111, 120
    directory, 72
    milk with, 65
    production of, 48
    sugar with, 66
chairs, teas and, 86
chanoyu ceremony, 91
Cherry Lane, 1
China
    Opium Wars with, 19–20
    tea ceremonies, 91–92
    tea plantations in, 29
    white tea in, 38
Chinese tea eggs, 109, 115
Contents Homeware, 1–2
cooking with tea, 109–128
Crome, Bruce, 6–7, 9
customers, become increasingly adventurous, 8

Darjeeling tea, 17, 29
Dodd, John, 30
drinking tea, 79
dry leaf, defined, 34
drying of tea leaves, 26–29, 33
'dust', 18

Earl Grey tea, 48
East India Company, given tea monopoly, 20–21
Egypt, tea ceremonies in, 93
Elliott, Charles, 20
Evi O., 150
experience calendars, 156

'fannings', 18
fermentation of leaves, 26–29
fine picking, 18
finish, defined, 34
Fitzroy store, 2, 5–6
flavonoids, 101, 103
flavoured teas, 48, 60–61, 72
flowering tea, 50
foods with tea, 82
fruit tisanes, 54

Gibbs, Courtney, 134
glasses, teas and, 87
Gong Fu brewing method, 91

grading of tea, 29
green tea
    brewing, 60–61
    directory, 71
    Green Tea Ice Cream, 119
    nutritional benefits, 101
    production of, 42
Grey, Lord, 48
growing and harvesting tea, 17, 25, 29
gunpowder tea, 29

HA Bennett & Sons, 5
hairstyles, teas and, 88
hand-crafted teas, 50, 61, 72
harvesting tea
    see growing and harvesting tea
Hassett, Theo, 137
health benefits of tea, 101–104
herbal tisanes, 54, 61, 72–73
Hong Kong, 92
House of Orange, 18
Hunan, yellow tea from, 40

iced teas, 66
Iggy & Lou Lou, 133, 149
India, tea ceremonies in, 93
Indian tea, 29
infusions (tisanes), 54
inspiration, 174
Isogawa, Akira, 133

Japan, tea ceremonies, 91, 93
Japanese tea, 31
jasmine blossoms, 56

Karlsson, Kristina, 144–147
Korea, tea ceremonies, 92

Lapsang Souchong tea, 56
Lapsang Souchong Tea Eggs, 115
leaf teas, 18
Lemongrass and Ginger tea, sugar with, 66
Lin Ze-xu, 19–20
lingers, defined, 34
Lipton, Thomas, 30
liquor, defined, 34

Manfield, Christine, 109
Matcha tea, 42, 109
medium picking, 18
milk with tea, 65
moods, teas for, 83
Morocco, tea ceremonies, 95
mouthfeel, defined, 34

Nelson, Olivia, 139
New York Breakfast tea, cooking with, 122
Newtown store, 7
notes, defined, 34

O'Connor, Jan, 1–2, 6–7
Odrowaz, Chris, 138
Oolong tea
    brewing, 60–61
    directory, 71
    nutritional benefits, 101
    production of, 44
Opium Wars, 19–20
Orange, House of, 18
orange pekoe grade, 18
oxidation of tea, 25–26, 32

picking tea, 17–18, 32
polyphenols, 101
Pomegranate Sunrise, 128
processing tea, 17–18, 25–26, 32–34

recipes using tea, 111–128
'red teas', 46

Robinson, Samantha, 133, 140–143
rolling of tea leaves, 26, 33
rooibos tea
    brewing, 61
    directory, 72
    production of, 52
    Rooibos Pumpkin Bites, 113
rose petals, 56
Russia, tea ceremonies, 95

scented teas, 56
Selzer, Irene and Peter, 133, 149
Sen no Rikyu (monk), 91
Shearer, Kirsten, author recruits, 7–9
Shearer, Maryanne (author), 1, 9
    family of, 6–7
    teapot collection, 79
sinensis varietal, 17
skin protection, 103
smoked teas, 56
South Africa, rooibos tea in, 52
Sri Lankan tea plantations, 30
St Kilda store, 6
steeped tea, 34
su-chong teas, 56
sugar with tea, 66
superfine picking, 18

T2 culture and experience,
    133, 154–156, 164
    history, 1–9
    milestones, 188–189
    reinvention of business, 8–9
    T2 Generation, 184
    T2 HQ, 166
Taiwanese tea, 30
Taylor, James, 30
tea
    bag vs loose, 68
    brewing, 58–63
    cooking with, 109–128
    drinking, 79
    fermenting, 26–29
    grading, 29
    growing and harvesting, 17, 25, 29
    health benefits of, 101–104
    matching, 81–89
    production, 17–18, 25–26, 32–34
    varieties, 17, 25, 32
tea bags, 68
tea ceremonies, 91–95
tea directory, 71–73
tea tasting wheel, 35
tea tastings at Fitzroy store, 5
'Tea Too Tea' brand, 5
tea wars, 19
temperature for brewing tea, 58–59
theanine, 101–102
times of day, teas for, 84
Tin & Ed, 151
tisanes, 54, 72–73 *see also* flavoured teas;
    herbal tisanes

Unilever acquires T2, 9

varieties of tea, 17, 25, 32
    see also tea directory
Veuve Clicquot Businesswoman
    of the Year award, 189

Water Leaf, 1
weight loss, 103
wet leaf, defined, 34
white tea, 38, 60, 71
withering of tea leaves, 26, 33

Xishuangbanna, 29

yellow tea, 40, 60, 71

LANTERN

UK | USA | Canada | Ireland | Australia
India | New Zealand | South Africa | China

Penguin Books is part of the Penguin Random House group of companies
whose addresses can be found at global.penguinrandomhouse.com.

Penguin
Random House
Australia

First published by Penguin Group (Australia), 2015

10 9 8 7 6 5 4 3 2 1

Design by Evi O. © Penguin Group (Australia)
Photography by Magenta Burgin, except pages 4 (left) and 7 by Richard Powers;
page 9 by Milk Group; pages viii, 12–13, 27–8, 78, 80–1, 96–7, 103, 108, 130, 158–9,
174, 177, 178–9 and 183 by Dan Crawford; pages 10–11, 157, 167, 168–9, 171 and 173
by Trevor Mein; pages 96–7 by Bryce Ford; page 162 (London) by Amelia Karlsen;
page 162 (New York) by Brian De Pinto; and pages 186–7 from T2 archive
Illustrations by Grace Mathis and Evi O.
Typeset in Harriet by Evi O.
Colour separation by Splitting Image Colour Studio, Clayton, Victoria
Printed and bound in China by 1010 Printing International Ltd

National Library of Australia
Cataloguing-in-Publication entry

Shearer, Maryanne, author.
T2 : the book / Maryanne Shearer.
9781921383625 (hardback)
Includes index.
T2 (Firm)
Tea--Australia.
Tearooms--Australia.
Tea trade--Australia.
Tea making paraphernalia.

641.33720994

penguin.com.au/lantern

T2™

Terrific Toffee
LOOSE LEAF FLAVOURED BLACK TEA

Net 250g | approx 75 cups

T2™

Red Green Vanilla
LOOSE LEAF FLAVOURED ROOIBOS TISANE

T2™

Turkish Apple & Cinnamon
INSTANT FLAVOURED TISANE

T2™

Strawberries & Cream
LOOSE LEAF FRUIT TISANE

Net 250g | approx 75 cups

T2™

Southern Sunrise
LOOSE LEAF FLAVOURED FRUIT TISANE

Net 250g / 8.8oz | approx 75 cups

T2™

Peppermint
LOOSE LEAF HERBAL TISANE

PROCESSOR 10683P
AUSTRALIAN
CERTIFIED
ORGANIC

31901059328072